E. R. (Elias Root) Beadle

The Old and the New, 1743-1876

The Second Presbyterian Church of Philadelphia

E. R. (Elias Root) Beadle

The Old and the New, 1743-1876
The Second Presbyterian Church of Philadelphia

ISBN/EAN: 9783337008239

Printed in Europe, USA, Canada, Australia, Japan

Cover: Foto ©Lupo / pixelio.de

More available books at **www.hansebooks.com**

The Old and the New.

1743-1876.

The Second Presbyterian Church

OF PHILADELPHIA.

Its Beginning and Increase.

BY

E. R. Beadle, Pastor.

—1876.—

CORRESPONDENCE.

*A*T *a meeting of the Ladies' Association of the Second Presbyterian Church, held at the Chapel, January 10th, 1877, the following Resolutions were adopted :—*

WHEREAS:—*The congregation having listened with great interest to the able and instructive historical discourses delivered by our Pastor, and knowing that there is a strong desire to possess the same in a permanent form, not only by the members of our own congregation, but also by many others who are interested in the subject : Therefore :—*

RESOLVED:—*That our Pastor be requested to allow this Society the privilege of publishing the same, and that a printed copy be presented to the Historical Society of the Presbyterian Church, in conformity with a Resolution of the General Assembly.*

RESOLVED:—*That a Committee be appointed to wait upon our Pastor with a copy of these Resolutions.*

HARRIET W. HODGE,
President.

SARAH P. SMITH,
Secretary.

JANUARY 10TH, 1877.

Committee appointed :—MRS. J. E. GRAEFF, MRS. HORACE PITKIN, MRS. F. W. HUBBELL.

212 SOUTH EIGHTH STREET,

January 13th, 1877.

MISS SARAH P. SMITH,
Secretary Ladies' Association :—

It gives me great pleasure to comply with the request of the Ladies' Association.

E. R. BEADLE.

TABLE OF CONTENTS.

———————

*STAND ye in the ways, and see, and ask for
"the old paths, where is the good way, and
"walk therein, and ye shall find rest for your
"souls."*—JEREMIAH vi.: 16.

———————

TO THE

OFFICERS, MEMBERS AND FRIENDS

OF THE

Second Presbyterian Church,

IN

PHILADELPHIA.

"Think on these things."

B

ON the third day of December, 1876, the Second Presbyterian Church of Philadelphia was one hundred and thirty-three years old. Its birth-day was celebrated by the commencement of these Sermons, which briefly tell the story of its life and work. The story passes to record, to embalm the memory of the mighty dead, and to give knowledge and cheer to those who shall in after times, inherit the trusts and bear the ark in this old and honored Church of Christ.

I.

Job viii.: 7, 8, 10.

" Though thy beginning was small, yet thy latter end should greatly increase.
" For inquire, I pray thee, of the former age, and prepare thyself to the search
" of their fathers : Shall they not teach thee, and tell thee, and utter words out
" of their heart ? "

THE roots of things lie far out of sight.   Causes may
be very remote, and great results flow from small
beginnings.   The mightiest rivers of our globe find
their source in basins that an ox might exhaust, or springs
that the careless eye would not detect.   In these words we
have an expression of a common sentiment and fact : — that
small beginnings often have large increase and issue in profound and wide-spread results.   This is eminently true of
sound principles and enterprises based upon benevolence and
truth.   Abraham entered Canaan with staff in hand, but his
seed became as the sand of the sea shore for multitude.   The

pilgrims were brought to this continent in a single ship, but the navies of the world could not transport their descendants.

The mystic seed of truth may be small as a mustard seed, but, like it, will grow into trees in whose branches the birds of heaven may light, or make forests from which cities shall be built. Cities rise and spread from the Indian's wigwam or the hunter's cabin. Churches grow from prayer meetings in a private house, or mission schools in a neglected neighborhood. The most powerful organizations have their infancy and growth. The beginning of the Second Church lies far back, and for its real origin we must inquire of the former age, and search among the fathers. The organized church life began in seventeen hundred and forty-three, but the causes which resulted in its organization must be sought still farther away.

In 1735 a young man, born in Gloucester, England, was found at Oxford, in close fellowship and earnest labors with the two Wesleys. These godly men were much in prayer together, and instant in evangelistic labors. They were exceptional men, and peculiar in their earnest zeal to awaken a deeper religious interest in the community, and to win souls for Christ. The Wesleys, while doing a great work in England, became also greatly interested in the American

Colonies, and both crossed the ocean to preach the gospel in the new settlements.

Whitefield, for the time, chose to remain in England, and was ordained by Bishop Benson in the Cathedral at Gloucester, June 20th, 1736, on which day he preached his first sermon at twenty-two years of age. He soon found his way to London, and two months from the time of his ordination preached his first sermon in the metropolis in Bishopsgate Church. On entering the pulpit the people smiled at his youthful appearance, and the common feeling seemed to be that the lad was much out of place ; but, as he proceeded in the sermon, the feeling changed, and people wondered, and asked who he was, and whence he came. As he came down he was greeted on every side, and invited to preach in other churches in the City. He accepted invitations, and preached in many places. A profound interest was awakened among all classes. Noble families attended, and followed him from church to church ; the streets were crowded which led to the churches where he was announced, and no house was large enough to hold the multitudes which thronged to hear him.

In the meantime the Wesleys were writing from Georgia, and urging him to sail for the new world. One of these urgent letters found him preaching to an illiterate people in

Hampshire. It was a stirring appeal for immediate departure for America, with promise of "food and raiment, a house to "lay his head in, and a crown of glory that fadeth not away." "Upon reading this (Whitefield says) my heart leaped within "me, as it were, and echoed to the call."

He soon sailed for Georgia, and landed at Savannah, where he at once began his favorite work. It was found advisable that he should be ordained as a priest, and for this he returned to England, and took orders at Oxford, January, 1739. In August following he was again on his way to America.

He landed this time at Philadelphia, and began to preach at once. No church then built could hold the crowds which pressed to hear him, and, had they been large enough, none were open to him. His fame as a new light minister and a field preacher had crossed the ocean before him, and both churches and preachers were afraid to give him welcome.

But houses in which to preach were not necessary. The old Court House standing on the corner of Second and Market streets had both steps and balcony, and these were his favorite preaching places. To this corner the crowds found their way, and often filled the street from the Court House to the Delaware. Franklin says :—"The multitudes of all sects and "denominations that attended his sermons were enormous."

Still another preaching place was on Society Hill, between Spruce and Pine, Second and Front streets. Here he took his stand by the flagstaff, and preached to fifteen thousand people. He preached often twice, and sometimes three times in a day, and on Sabbaths four times.

James Pemberton, a friend, writes : —

"Eleventh of 9th month, 1739. He preaches every day. "Some of our curious youths of rash judgment, who look "at words more than substance, are very constant in attend- "ance and much pleased. He preached three nights succes- "sively upon our Court House steps, on Second street, where "he exceedingly takes with the people. Last night he had "the greatest multitude I ever saw, and some accident hap- "pened which greatly frightened many. Some thought it was "an earthquake ; others that it was fire, and others that the "Spaniards were come. Many were hurt by falling, and "being trodden upon ; many lost their hats, cloaks, etc. The "preacher had to leave off speaking till they recovered their "senses, which some did and others did not. His intentions "are good, but. he has not arrived at such perfection as to see "as far as he yet may."

James Logan, at a later date, says : —

" None can be long a stranger to George Whitefield. All I
" have to say of him is, that by good language, a better utter-
" ance, an engaging manner, and a powerful voice, he gained
" much at first on most sorts of people. He gained so much
" on the multitude that they have begun for him a great brick
" building in which, though not covered, he preached a great
" many times." * " It must be confessed his preaching has
" a good effect in reclaiming many dissolute people, but from
" his countenancing so very much the most hot-headed pre-
" destinarians, and those of them, principally, who had been
" accounted by the more sober as little better than madmen,
" he and they have actually driven divers into despair, and
" some into perfect madness. In short, it is apprehended by
" the more judicious that the whole will end in confusion, to
" the great prejudice of the cause of virtue and solid religion ;
" his doctrine turning on the danger of good works without
" such a degree of sanctifying faith as comes up to his
" gauge."

The effects of his preaching were seen not only (as friend
Logan says) " in reclaiming many dissolute people," but the
whole tone of society was changed.

Franklin says : —

"It was wonderful to see the change soon made in the
"manners of our inhabitants. From being thoughtless and
"indifferent about religion it seemed as if all the world was
"growing religious ; so that one could not walk through the
"town in an evening without hearing psalms sung in different
"families in every street."

Public amusements were repressed ; the dancing school
was discontinued ; the ball and concert room shut up, and
when some gay and spirited young men broke open the
room, and announced a ball, there was not a single person who would attend. Significant notices are scattered
through the accounts of the times. " Religious conversation
"became general." " Religious books only would sell."

Whitefield himself says of these remarkable preaching seasons : —

" Many people and many ministers weep. My own soul
" is much carried out. I preached to a vast assembly of
" sinners ; nearly twelve thousand were collected, and I had
" not spoken long before I perceived numbers melting. As I
"proceeded the power increased, and thousands cried out.

" Never before did I see such a glorious sight. Oh ! what
"strong crying and tears were poured forth after the dear
" Lord Jesus."

Not only was this powerful influence felt among the crowds
gathered in the streets, but multitudes sat in boats on the
river, and felt the power of his searching appeals. When
preaching at Society Hill he was heard to utter the gospel
call at Gloucester, two miles away. Some persons came
twenty miles on foot to hear him, and one memorable case of
conversion took place of a lady who had made such a journey.

When preaching once on the Court House steps, a lad who
held the lantern was so overcome that he let the lantern fall,
and this probably caused the confusion of which friend Pemberton speaks. It was John Rogers, who became a Presbyterian minister, and was Moderator of the First General
Assembly in America, at its first meeting, held in the Second
Presbyterian Church, Third and Arch streets.

The religious interest excited by the preaching of Whitefield
continued for a long time though he did not remain long in
Philadelphia. His destination was Georgia, and when he left
the City one hundred and fifty gentlemen accompanied him to
Chester, where he preached to thousands who gathered at his

coming. At White Clay Creek he preached to eight thousand people, of whom nearly three thousand were on
horseback.

In 1740 Whitefield was again in Philadelphia. In the meantime Gilbert Tennent appeared upon the stage. Full of the
Holy Ghost and of faith, this eminent preacher and successful
winner of souls carried forward the work. They now, for a
time, labored together in the Kingdom of God, gathering
multitudes as reapers sweep down the harvest ripe for the
sickle. When Whitefield was called again to leave Philadelphia he committed the work to Tennent's hands.

At this time the First Presbyterian Church (now worshipping on Washington square) was in existence, and occupied a
house on High street (now Market), built in 1704. Of this
congregation it is said : —

"They continued in peace and increase until the time of
"the Rev. George Whitefield, when a party drew off under
"the name of 'new lights.'" It is probable that from the
many converts some connected themselves with that congregation, and also with churches of other denominations in the
City ; but converts were so multiplied that a new organization
became a necessity, and in December, 1743, one hundred and
forty persons, after most careful examination, made a public

profession of their faith in Christ, and were organized as the
Second Presbyterian Church in Philadelphia.

The original Charter granted to this church is in existence,
and its closing sentences are these : —

"*Thomas Penn and John Penn, true and absolute proprietaries of the Pro-*
"*vince of Pennsylvania and Counties of New Castle, Kent, and Sussex, on*
"*Delaware, to all persons to whom these presents may come, Greeting :—*

   *   *   *   *   *   *   *

"Wherefore they have prayed us to incorporate the committee of said church,
"by the name of the Trustees of the Second Presbyterian Church of the City of
"Philadelphia, in the Province of Pennsylvania; and that they and their suc-
"cessors, by such name, may be erected and constituted a body politic and
"corporate, and have perpetual succession. Now know ye, that we, favoring the
"prayer and application of the said elders, deacons, and members, and willing
"as much as in us lies to encourage virtue, piety, and charity, and for other
"good causes and considerations us thereto specially moving, have nominated,
"ordained and appointed Samuel Smith, Andrew Hodge, John Redman, Hugh
"McCulloch, William Shippen, sr., William Henry, William Shippen, jr., Nathan
"Cooke, Gunning Bedford, John Bayard, Jedediah Snowden, Joseph Reed,
"William Hollingshead, William Carson, John Hall, William Bradford, Robert
"Harris, John Rhea, Isaac Snowden, Jonathan B. Smith, Benjamin Armitage,
"William Drury, Benjamin Harbison, and David Chambers, to be the first
"Trustees of the Second Presbyterian Church, in the City of Philadelphia."

Gilbert Tennent was chosen the first pastor. He did not at once accept the call. In the meantime, Dr. Finley, from Princeton College, supplied the congregation. Before entering upon his labors as pastor of the Second Church, Tennent made a tour through New England, preaching by the way, and principally in the larger towns. He preached many times, and with great success, in Boston. It was a winter of extreme cold, so intense that Long Island Sound was frozen over. Like Whitefield, he had a powerful voice, and preached with great earnestness. Great multitudes were converted.

Dr. Cutler, of Boston, says : —

"Gilbert Tennent afflicted us more than the intense cold "and snow." "While Whitefield was here the town was, as "it were, in a siege. The streets were crowded with coaches "and chaises. He lashed and anathematized the Church of " England. After him came one Tennent, a minister, impu- " dent and saucy, and told them they were damned. This "charmed them, and in the dreadfullest winter I ever saw, "people wallowed in the snow, day and night, for the benefit "of his beastly brayings."

At New Haven, Tennent preached to a great crowd. A young man, who was a student in Yale College, heard him, and was converted.   It was James Sproat, who became afterwards the third pastor of the Second Presbyterian Church.

When Tennent returned from New England he entered upon his pastoral work.   He lived at that time at Bedminster, "a "neat country place, having a fine collection of fruit trees."   It was out of town, and advertised as a "very rural and agree- "able place."   It was at the corner of Fourth and Wood streets.   Tennent commenced his work with great zeal and earnestness, and was instant in labors.   He preached often, and visited almost daily from house to house.   So many distressed souls were to be seen that his feet were actually

blistered in his constant walking from place to place.

The "large brick building," which the multitude had begun for Whitefield, was finished by subscription.   It was called "the new building," and afterwards the "Old Academy," and stood in

THE OLD ACADEMY.

Fourth street, below Arch. It was "large" for those times, and presented a modest, church-like appearance. We reproduce it on the opposite page : —

The conditions upon which the subscriptions were given were, that the building should be for the " free use of itinerant "preachers forever, as well as for the promulgation of the "peculiar tenets and religious views called ' new light.' "

Peter Kalm, a Swede, who traveled in America in 1751, says of these peoples and their tenets : —

"By the name of New Lights, are understood the people who have, from " different religions, became proselytes to the well known Whitefield. * * * " The proselytes of this man, or the " New Lights," are at present merely a sect " of Presbyterians ; for, though Whitefield was originally a clergyman of the " English Church, yet he deviated little by little from her doctrines, and on "arriving, in the year 1744, at Boston, New England, he disputed with the " Presbyterians about their doctrines so much that he almost entirely embraced "them ; for Whitefield was no great disputant, and could therefore be easily led "by these cunning people whithersoever they would have him. This, also, " during his latter stay in America, caused his audiences to be less numerous "than during the first. The New Lights built first, in the year 1741, a great " house in the western part of the town, to hold divine service in. But a division "arising amongst them afterwards, and besides on other accounts, the building "was sold to the town in 1749 or '50, and destined for a school. The New " Lights then built a church, which I call the new Presbyterian one."

C

In 1753 the "Old Academy" was made the College of
Philadelphia ; in 1779 it became the University of Pennsylvania, and in 1875 was reproduced in somewhat enlarged
dimensions and more elaborate structure on the west bank
of the Schuylkill, at the corner of Locust and Thirty-sixth
streets.

In this "new building" the Second Church worshipped for
nine years (1741—1750). In 1749, the building having been
purchased for the first Academy of Philadelphia, notice was
given to the congregation that they must procure some other
place of worship, and that they could have three years to
secure a suitable site. A strong committee was appointed to
find a proper location. After much search and some delay,
the lot on the north-west corner of Third and Arch streets
was fixed upon, and purchased. On this lot a house was
built. It stood eighty feet on Arch street, and sixty feet on
Third street. It was built of brick, and a wooden steeple
was afterwards put up on the west end, and paid for by a
lottery. This wooden steeple was the cause of much gossip
and some unpleasant feeling. There was but one other in the
City, and the chronicler says : —

"The Episcopalians having no mind to see their architectural
beauties rivaled, expressed their sentiments in these lines :"—

> " The Presbyterians built a church,
>   And fain would build a steeple :
> We think it may become the church,
>   But not become the people."

The steeple was afterwards taken down, not because unbe-
coming either to church or people, but because it was thought
to be unsafe. The front entrance to the building was on
Third street, and the pulpit was placed on the north side.
Over it hung a large sounding-board, suspended in such a
way as to cause some anxiety among the younger worshippers
lest it should fall on the preacher's head. Below the pulpit,
and directly in front, was a reading desk for the precentor, or
as he was then called, "the setter of tunes." Mr. Joseph
Eastburn performed this duty with great earnestness and zeal,
and for a long time with great acceptance. He was afterwards ordained as an evangelist, and ministered to the first
church for seamen established in Philadelphia, and perhaps in
the country. An aisle ran through the middle of the church
from east to west, and another from north to south, paved
with brick, in which were placed slabs to commemorate the
dead who were buried underneath. The pews were square
and high, painted white, and mounted with a mahogany rail.
One pew was set aside as the President's or the Governor's

pew. It was surmounted by a canopy, supported by carved columns.

Provisions were also made for the Members of Congress, as the following, from John Adams, the second President of the United States, pleasantly acknowledges : —

"PHILADELPHIA, *January 5, 1791.*

"SIR:

"I received this morning the letter you did me the honor to write me, "communicating the resolution of the Second Presbyterian Church, in Arch "street, of the 29th ultimo, appropriating the large pew fronting the pulpit, and "the two pews adjoining it, for the use of the Vice-President of the United "States, and such Members of both Houses of Congress as chose, during their "sessions, to worship in that church, and immediately communicated it and the "resolution enclosed in it by reading both in the Senate of the United States. "Permit me, Sir, to express to you and to the Corporation my thanks for obliging "mark of their respectful attention to

"Your and their most obedient and most humble servant,

"JOHN ADAMS.

"MR. JOHN REDMAN,
"*President of the Corporation of the Second*
"*Presbyterian Church in Arch street.*"

Under the singer's gallery was hung a glass chandelier (now in the possession of this church), which was purchased from the effects of Washington when he removed from

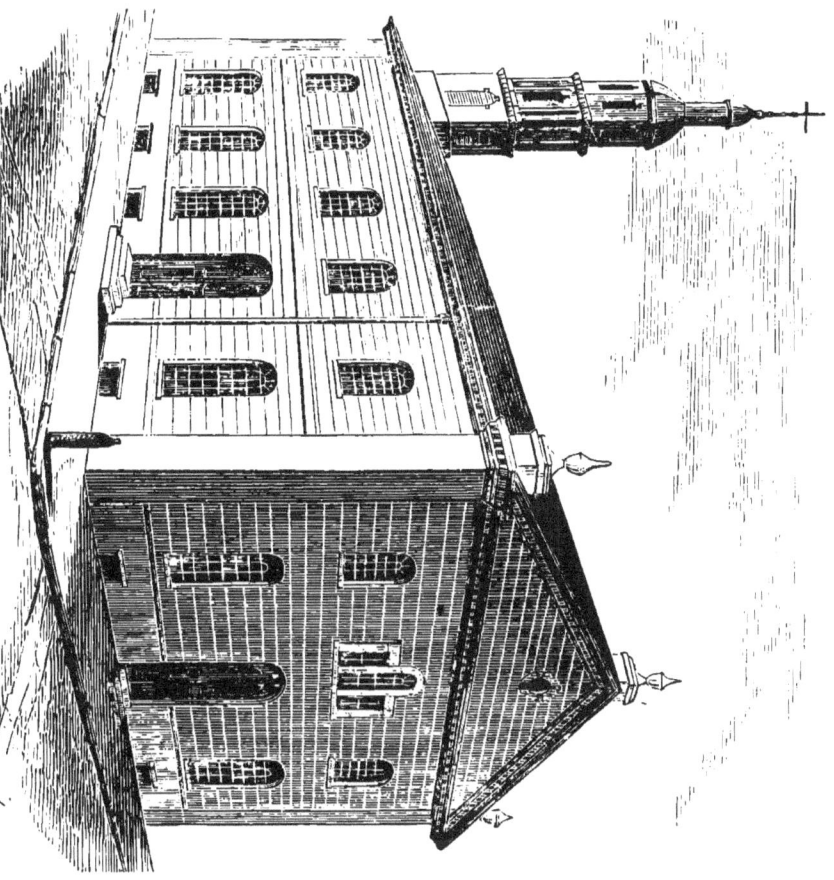

CHURCH THIRD AND ARCH:—Built in 1750.

Philadelphia.   This chandelier became an object of much interest, and in Peter Lesley's time it is said : —

"People worshipping there often stopped to see it, and he "had much trouble to keep them from taking off the drops "to carry away as mementos."

No provisions were made for the comfortable heating of the church, and ladies "were in the habit of having foot-stoves "brought to keep their feet warm."

Mr. Samuel Hazard says : —

"I have frequently carried one of these to church for my "mother;" and he describes them as "small square boxes, "made of wood and tin, perforated with holes, in which was "placed a small vessel containing hot coals."

Hot bricks, also, wrapped in carpeting, were brought for the comfort of hands or feet in the cold season.

The church was lighted by candles in the chandelier, and in sconces placed along the wall.   The exterior of the building was rough-cast, and had a "long, narrow, barn-like appearance, without any architectural beauty."   We present it here as it appeared with the steeple.*

This building suffered much during the occupancy of the

* See page 29.

British in 1778. The pews and woodwork were destroyed, and the fence around the church removed. A large brass chandelier, or "branch," as it was called, which had been imported from England, was taken away, and sold in New York. It was afterwards recovered from the purchaser.

An old bill for damages has been found. The vouchers have disappeared.

"The following are the sums paid to repair damages done the Second Presby-"terian Church, and the cost of some things destroyed in 1778, when the British "army lay in Philadelphia : —

	£	s.	d.
"Paid removing the pews, ...	22	2	6
"1778, Dec. 19th. — Repairs, £229 0s. 3d., (Exchangè, six for "one,)	38	3	4½
"1779, April 1st. — For do. paid, £442 17s. 6d., (Exchange, "seventeen for one,)	26	1	0½
"1779, March 25th. — Do. paid, £343 7s. 9d., (at ten for one,) .	34	7	9
"Paid fencing in the grave yard, ...	7	5	10½
"Cost of the chandelier destroyed, ...	74	9	0
	£202	9	7

"We do certify the above account of damages and repairs, as above stated, is "just and true as stated, and are supported by the inclosed vouchers.

"JOHN STILLÉ,

"*April 30, 1783.*"   "PAINE NEWMAN."

As the location at Third and Arch streets was in the busy part of the town, the passage of vehicles much disturbed the congregation in their worship, and a memorial was presented to the City authorities, praying for relief. The memorial is as follows : —

" To the Mayor, Aldermen, and Common Council of Philadelphia, the Mem-
" orial of the Trustees of the Second Presbyterian Church, in the said City,
" respectfully showeth : —

" That your memorialists are very much disturbed in their public worship on "the Sabbath, by the frequent passing and re-passing of carriages during the "time of divine service; and they therefore pray that they may be permitted to "fix chains at the corner of Mulberry and Third streets, on the Sabbath, for so "long time as may be necessary to prevent similar interruptions in future.

" And your memorialists, etc.

" August 6, 1795."

The request was not granted, but the Legislature passed a law authorizing the use of chains, and on every Sabbath morning, when the service began, the sexton stretched the chains across both Arch and Third streets. This plan stopped the passage of vehicles to and fro, and prevented the disturbance of the worship, but did not work altogether satisfactorily. Horsemen would go around the chains, and the clattering upon the pavement could be distinctly heard inside. This also was at length stopped, as the sexton and the constable in charge were authorized to arrest persons attempting to infringe or evade the law.

Sacramental occasions were seasons of unusual solemnity and interest. On the evening preceding the administration of the Lord's Supper the minister and elders distributed to the church members small pieces of metal, called "tokens," on one side of which was impressed a heart. These tokens were taken up on the morning of the communion in pewter plates, now in the possession of the church, and marked "church "pewter." They are stamped with the words "made in "London," and some of them bear monograms of "J. D. D." Communicants partook of the sacrament from tables spread in the aisles. The colored communicants were served by themselves, in pews in the western aisle. Tables were used until it became necessary to enlarge the church, when the fronts of pews were so made as to let down, and thus furnish a table for those sitting in the pews.

The appearance of the congregations in those early times is also noted. Watson says : —

"The Episcopalians showed most grandeur in dress and "costume; next, the Presbyterians, the gentlemen of whom "freely indulged in powdered and frizzled hair. Among the

CHURCH, THIRD AND ARCH STREETS:—Enlarged in 1809.

" Methodists there were no powdered heads of men, and no
" gay bonnets or ribbons were to be seen among them."

In 1809 it was found that the congregation needed more
room, and it was concluded to extend the building and embrace the ground occupied by the base of the steeple. The
steeple itself had been taken down. This made a complete
change in the pews and the pulpit. The pulpit was moved to
the west end, ornamented with some carving, and painted
white. The pews were modernized and cushioned. Glass
chandeliers were introduced in place of the sconces on the
wall. A lecture room was added in 1819.

In order to gain a clear understanding of the early history
of our church we must glance at the state of the City in those
early times. In 1726 a man going from the Old Swedes'
Church to the " Blue Horse Tavern " (now Ninth and South
streets), saw nothing but lofty forests, swamps, and abundant
game. Between High street and Arch, and Fifth and Sixth
streets, was " Hudson's orchard," an enclosure " rented for
" eight dollars per annum for a horse pasture." Near the
corner of Fifth and High streets was a pond, where the City
boys skated in winter and resorted for wild fowl shooting in
summer. When the Second Church built its house at the
corner of Third and Arch, the land was taken up from

Samuel Preston Moore and Richard Hill, on a ground-rent of
£24 12s. 6d., sterling, per annum. The lot was ninety-eight
and a half feet on Arch street, and eighty on Third street.
The land was used as a farm, and when the house was put
up it was known as the "new meeting-house in Dr. Hill's
"pasture."

Up to 1793, wealthy merchants lived over their stores in
Water and Front streets ; but about this time some venturous
men began to extend the western limits of the City. Mr.
Markoe, a man of remarkable enterprise, built a house on
High street (now Market), between Ninth and Tenth, "in a
"meadow," and so remote from all City intercourse that his
friends made his enterprise a jest, and said, "he lived out on
"High street, next door but one to the Schuylkill ferry." West
of Tenth no streets were opened or thought of by the most
adventuresome. Frog ponds and a few brick kilns were the
most common sights, and when a few families made a bold
push, and struck out into the wilderness above Tenth street,
it was a matter of common sympathy and regret that, "gen-
"teel families should encounter so many inconveniences to
"make western improvements." This was the beginning of
"going west" in this latitude. The two boldest innovators
of that time were a Mr. Wahn and a Mr. Sims. The first

ventured to brave public opinion, and took a grand stride to
Seventh and Chestnut. His friend, inspired by his courage,
overran him, and built at Ninth and Chestnut.

In 1835, after the building at Third and Arch had been
occupied for eighty-three years, it was thought desirable to
remove to a more eligible position. A committee was appointed to make sale of the property, and procure a new site
for the church. As usual, on changing church locations,
there was much difference of opinion. Some wished to go
into Fourth street, and others into Seventh. No small opposition was made to the Seventh street location, on account of
its being "too far west." Differences were at length, however,
reconciled, and the committee purchased two lots on Seventh,
near Arch. Messrs. Kane, Chauncey, Strawbridge, Freeland,
and Hazard, were appointed a building committee. The
corner stone for the new building was laid by the pastor,
Rev. Dr. Cuyler, September 6, 1836.

Dr. Green made an address, in which he sets forth the
reasons for removing from Third and Arch to Seventh streets.
He says : —

"The structure which, under the blessing of God, will, it is hoped, rise over
"the corner-stone which has now been deposited, has been rendered indispen-
"sable by the repeal of that law of this State which authorized the placing of

" chains across the streets of this City, opposite to the churches, during the hours
" of public worship, on the Lord's day. The house, which its owners and
" occupants have thus been compelled to abandon, was always unfavorably
" located for the preservation of that entire quiet, so exceedingly desirable in the
" worship of Almighty God. The late Dr. Elias Boudinot, whose father was
" among the original members of this congregation, informed me that Dr.
" Franklin advised the people who built that house, by no means to place it at
" the corner of two streets; but to seek a location for it in the centre of a square,
" not then difficult to be found, or expensive in the purchase. Franklin's
" sagacious mind foresaw, that although at that time the population of the City
" and the use of carriages, gave little interruption to the service of the sanctuary,
" it would be far otherwise in process of time.

   " Since the removal of the street chains, the increase of carriages, and the
" introduction of a new vehicle — the omnibus, the most noisy of all — and all
" this connected with the increased and increasing disregard and desecration of
" the Sabbath, the church at the corner of Third and Mulberry, or Arch streets,
" is certainly in as unfit a location for the public worship of God as could be
" found in the City. Wherefore, the brethren have done well in seeking a place
" for a christian temple in which their devotions and religious instruction may
" be conducted without being marred, as they have been to a lamentable extent,
" for a considerable time past, in the house where they now assemble.   In taking
" this step, they doubtless violate some tender feelings. The house where their
" fathers worshipped, in which many of them have been baptized, and have often
" heard the messages of salvation, and held sweet communion in sacred ordin-
" ances — cannot but be associated with recollections, at once solemn, impressive,
" and delightful. But there can be no equivalent for composure in prayer and
" praise, and for edification in listening to the dispensation of the gospel of the

"grace of God: and most auspicious it is, and highly creditable to all concerned,
"that it has been, as I am informed, with entire unanimity that this measure has
"been adopted, of abandoning a house in which spiritual edification is interfered
"with, and the erection of another, where this inestimable blessing may be fully
"enjoyed. May this harmony continue, as the best presage that every anticipa-
"tion of future benefits may be realized and exceeded."

This building was made of marble. The pulpit was also
of marble, and had behind it the tablet to the memory of
Whitefield and Tennent, which is now placed in our chapel
on Twenty-first street. It was lighted with gas, and probably
the first church so lighted in the City. The fixtures in our
chapel are a part of the old furniture. John Struthers (the
father of the late William Struthers, whose mementos are
in this beautiful baptismal fount, and some of these small
columns), was the architect. The church was dedicated July
16, 1837. Three sermons were preached on that occasion :
Dr. Cuyler in the morning, Dr. Green in the afternoon, and
Dr. Janeway in the evening.

Of the music in the Second Church, Mr. Samuel Hazard
writes : —

"The subject of psalmody and music has often been agitated in the congrega-
"tion. In 1763, a contest arose respecting the introduction of Watts' Psalms
"in place of the old Scotch version, when it was decided to adopt the former,
"in consequence of which one or two members withdrew from the church.

D

" Some years later, another contest arose respecting the giving out the line, as
" had been the practice, when it was decided to be omitted, and the congregation
"to provide themselves with books. The question also arose at another time,
" after the introduction of the organ, between the Trustees and Session, as to the
" right of the Session to direct the selection of tunes, which was referred to the
" Presbytery."

" There have since been other discussions with regard to church music."

Of the music in the new church he says : —

" It having become necessary, during the progress of the new building, to
" provide for the location of an organ in it, and to ascertain the sentiments of the
" congregation on the subject of introducing one; and there being some diversity
" of opinion, a meeting of pew-holders and communicants was called in the
" lecture-room in Cherry street, at which meeting it was decided in favor of
" having an organ, and the building committee were desired to prepare a suitable
" place for one. At this meeting, it is believed, only two persons raised their
" voices against the measure; one of them is deceased, and the other now be-
" longs to another church."

We have now passed rapidly over ninety years and more
of the history of the Second Church, touching for the present
only the salient points, and saying no more than was necessary to keep the thread of its history unbroken, and the
manner of its life steadily before us. Much remains. It will
be told in good time.

We have learned at least this much : —

I.

That the foundations of the Second Church were laid by God-fearing men.

It was born of spiritual necessities, and in spiritual throes, and baptized of the Holy Ghost. It took its place in the infant city as one of the strongholds of Zion, and opened its doors for the multitudes to come and worship God. It built on no uncertain ground. Its members were reproachfully called "new lights," because they stood manfully for the doctrines of the Reformation in the midst of widespread formalism and looseness of life. As we shall see in the end, it gave largely in benefactions, and multiplied so greatly that five Presbyterian churches grew out of its life, and remain to this day.

II.

It was a great power in the city and the land.

It drew to its organization and worship the highest families of the City. It was a power in political circles and social life.

It stood so high in the Presbyterian denomination that the
first General Assembly ever held in the United States con-
vened in its building. Its power was felt in moulding the
taste, and ordering the lives of the early citizens of Philadelphia, and we feel to this hour the influences for good which
were started by the old Second Presbyterian Church.

Founders of states, cities, and churches are to be highly
honored. The men who laid the foundations of this church
in those early days are to be held in sacred remembrance.
They lived in rude times, and built amid inconveniences and
hardships, not always forecasting the results of their labors,
or dreaming to what their small beginning would grow in its
increase, they labored for their own time, and fought the
battles of their day. They stood for God and the truth.
Trained in the doctrines and practice of sturdy old Presbyterians, whose life and blood came from Scotland and the
north of Ireland, they were the men who stood foremost in
the defence of civil and religious liberty. Its Presbyterian
blood runs in every vein of this Republic. Men of stern
principle, strong faith, simple habits, and iron will, the forest
went down before them, and enemies were driven from the
soil. A city grew under their hands, filled with schools, and
churches, and prosperous trade. They made the wilderness

blossom with their patient labor, and the city glad with their saintly lives. They trod the rough places before us, and smoothed the path for our coming. They have passed to their reward, and we enter into their labors. It is ours to perpetuate their memory, to conserve the interests which were so dear to them, and pass down our trusts unimpaired to the men and the generations who shall come after us.

II.

Micah ii.: 10.

"Arise ye, and depart, for this is not your rest."

WE cannot abide in one stay. We journey from place to place, pass from one condition to another. Growth, development, advance, are laws of our being. Times and seasons pass over us. We are children, then men, and in all the changes which mark our lives as the years come and go, we find the presence and force of this law of renewal. Vegetable life will eventually exhaust the soil, and must be transplanted to new fields. So we exhaust the resources of our location, or changes come about in our surroundings which compel a removal. God has implanted a necessity in our being that our characters should be formed by progressive acts, and our attainments reached through a series of changes and long lines of steady advance. Abram is to become the father of a great nation, and so he must arise, and depart from his native country, and go to a land of which he shall be told. The Puritans must be harried out of England, and find their way to the wilds of the western world, to test their principles, perfect their character, and make a highway for the nations. Their descendants in time must press their way from the coast to the interior, and from inland cities and fields to a farther West, and from the West itself to the shores of the Pacific and the ends of the earth.

We are constantly coming to new departures. Transition is the order of human life. There must be a succession of habitudes, employments, and estates. Rarely do men live and die in the dwellings where they were born. The dwellings remain, but the dwellers are scattered, and build new homes for themselves and their children. And what is true of individuals and families is true of communities and churches. The little settlements on the Delaware must grow into a city. The churches which were gathered in the infant colonies, and worshipped in log huts, with rude conveniences, must keep step with the march of migrating peoples, and build nobler houses of worship, as the people increase in numbers, and improvements in society demand better accommodations.

So the Second Church in its early history built for the time.
It was a small beginning, but it was quite abreast of the age,
and met the necessities of the people, who needed accommodations for stated religious worship.   For nine years they
worshipped in the Old Academy, and for eighty-three years
they occupied the building erected at Third and Arch, while
the City slowly extended its western limits, and steadily increased in population.   In this time Gilbert Tennent had his
pastorate of twenty one years, from 1743 to 1764.*   He was
succeeded by John Murray, who remained but a single year.
A vacancy of three years followed, when James Sproat, who
was converted under one of Tennent's sermons at New Haven,
while a student in college, was called, and commenced his
labors in March, 1769.   In December, 1787, Dr. Ashbel
Green was called as co-pastor with Dr. Sproat.   In 1793 Dr.

* During his ministry he manifested great interest in the people who began to cluster around
the lands in the northern part of the settlement. Many of them were brought under his
ministry, and he labored earnestly to propagate the gospel in these regions, then so remote
from city life and church privileges. Nothing was done, however, towards establishing a
church in the Northern Liberties until after the Revolution, and after the death of Mr. Tennant
in 1764. Dr. Sproat, in 1769, instituted regular religious services at Campington (corner of
Second and Coates), in a small house which the 2nd Church provided. During the war the
services were suspended, and the house used for military stores When peace was declared,
the project of gathering a congregation at Campington was revived, but took no definite
form until 1783, when Dr Green became the co-pastor with Dr. Sproat. The two pastors
alternated in the services of the church in the City and the preaching at Campington. This
was the beginning of the first Presbyterian church in the Northern Liberties, now under the
pastoral care of the Rev. Dr. Shepherd. It was the first-born of the Second Church.

Sproat died of yellow fever, after a pastorate of twenty-four years. A year later Rev. Mr. Abeel was called as assistant-pastor to Dr. Green. He remained but a year and a half, and then removed to New York. Four years later (1799) Dr. Jacob J. Janeway was called as co-pastor with Dr. Green. Dr. Green continued in service till 1812, when he was called to the College of New Jersey, and closed a pastorate of twenty-eight years. The next year the Rev. Thomas S. Skinner was called, as co-pastor with Dr. Janeway, and remained in the service until the autumn of 1816. Dr. Janeway continued the sole pastor till July, 1828, when he was called to the Western Theological Seminary at Alleghany, having finished a pastorate of twenty-nine years.

This resignation left the church vacant. Rev. Joseph Sanford was called in September of the same year, and remained in office till December, 1831. After Mr. Sanford's death a vacancy occurred for two years, when Rev. Cornelius C. Cuyler was called, and entered upon his work November 25, 1833. He remained for sixteen years, and in 1850 resigned. Rev. Charles W. Shields was then called, and settled in the same year. He remained until 1865, when he resigned, and the present pastor was called.

For seventy years the history of the Second Church ran

smoothly.   It held an honored place in the city, and was an
unquestioned power for good in the land.   Many of the
noblest families were recorded among its members, and found
regularly with its worshippers.   The dignity and manly bearing of its eldership have come down to us in many household
traditions.   They were men whose word passed in business
circles like lawful coin of the realm, greatly respected by all
classes, and highly venerated by the younger members of the
church and congregation.

A change began in 1813.   The coming of Mr. Skinner was
the signal for a new departure.   But twenty-two years of age,
possessed of unusual talent, a vivid imagination, and fervent
piety, with extraordinary command of language, and pleasing
address, his preaching was in striking contrast with the more
solemn, stately, and didactic administrations to which the
church had been so long accustomed.   His services were
always impressive, sometimes tender and pathetic as he
poured forth the invitations and promises of the gospel, and
again terrible and startling as he uttered the threatenings
of the law.   Great excitement followed.   The congregation
was much moved, and difference of feeling became unmistak-
ably apparent.   It was thought by some that the doctrines
preached were not altogether orthodox, and it was not long

before this undefined feeling took form, and the more prominent doctrines heard from the pulpit were characterized as
"new school." Discussions arose also about the use of
means or "measures," as they were called. Suspicions were
aroused. Sermons were watched and criticised. Sharp discussions followed. Eldership and families took sides, some
with the junior pastor, and others against him.

At this point in the history of the church, where, for the
first time, two seas met, we find the beginning of those con-
troversies which ended not only in the resignation of Mr.
Skinner, but in later times in the division of the Presbyterian
church into New and Old School. This disturbed condition
of things could not continue, and after a co-pastorate with
Dr. Janeway for three years and four months, in November,
1816, his relations with the church were dissolved. He
retired with twelve or fifteen families of his most devoted
friends and adherents, to a building in Locust street, above
Eighth, standing on the site of the present Musical Fund
Hall. He soon removed to Arch street, above Tenth, where
his friends erected for him the building which still stands, and
is occupied by the Fifth Presbyterian Church.*

* This was the second child of the Second Church.

At this time, the Second Church stood in the foremost rank
of Presbyterian churches in the land, and in some respects
might have been counted the very first. It was widely known
for its "intelligence, orthodoxy, influence, and wealth." In
ecclesiastical standing it had no peer, and in ecclesiastical
affairs its voice was powerful, if not absolute. But this apparently small division produced a profound shock. It was the
letting out of waters, and none could tell whither they would
come in their flow. The sharp contests which began here
spread into other churches, and to some extent affected the
entire religious community. Topics involving the propriety
of calling men "sinners," rather than "brethren;" of instruct-
ing unconverted people to pray, and permitting lay brethren
to preach, were everwhere discussed. They were heard in
the streets, in family circles, in neighborhood gatherings,
found their way into Church Sessions, Presbyteries, and
Synods, and finally to the General Assembly itself.

For twelve years after this disruption, the church held on
its way under the sole care of Dr. Janeway. When he left
for the Seminary at Allegheny, Rev. Joseph Sanford succeeded him. He was also young, and came with no small
reputation as a preacher and pastor. For a time his preaching
was acceptable and well attended. The hope was cherished

that with the new and eloquent pastor all the old difficulties
would be smoothed over and soon forgotten. A strong effort
was made to re-unite the members of the church and congregation in common efforts and interest for increased measures of prosperity and success. Everything promised well,
and for a time all seemed well, but the old leaven still existed,
though kept out of sight. Gradually it found its way to the
surface, and at last was revealed in its full strength. A portion of the congregation began to manifest decided disaffection
and impatience, while others were equally demonstrative in
their admiration and devotion to the young pastor. How far
the old difficulties were perpetuated, or what coloring and
force they gave to these divisions, it is impossible now to
tell. The troubles increased, however, rather than diminished. Disaffection grew, and became more pronounced, until
the church and congregation were divided into two distinct
and irreconcilable parties. The elders and leading members
of the church arrayed themselves on one side or the other.
Efforts were made openly by one party to remove the pastor,
and these were met by counter efforts to retain him.

At this juncture Mr. Sanford sickened and died. He was
buried from the church, and when the funeral services were
over the friends of the buried pastor, led by such excellent

men as Alexander Henry, Matthew Newkirk, Matthew Bevan, and others, retired and organized a new church. This became the Central Church, which is now worshiping at Eighth and Cherry streets, under the pastoral care of Rev. James Munro. This was the third child of the Second Church, born in spiritual throes and agonies, which took hold upon the very life.

Though these unhappy differences ended in a final separation, still the Christian feeling and affection seemed not altogether to have been destroyed. At the close of this year, ending April 1, 1833, the Trustees of the Second Church report : —

"That owing to the unhappy difference of sentiment and "alienation of brotherly feeling, which has been permitted to "arise and gain an ascendancy, uncontrolled by the mild "voice of reason or religion, a secession of several of the "pew-owners, pew-holders, and communicants, had taken "place."

But to show the kindly feeling and generous course pursued towards the seceding members, the report states that the "Board had voted the sum of two thousand dollars to "the widow of the late pastor;" they had also repaid in every instance to the seceding pew-owners the prices they had

originally paid for the same, and had paid also "to Matthew
" Newkirk, on behalf of teachers of the Sabbath School, the
" sum of two hundred and five dollars, for the library books
" left by them in the room." The report closes with con-
gratulations for the "unanimity and peace which prevail
" among them, and the prospect of an early settled ministry,"
and praying that "they might continue to do unto others
" as they would wish others to do to them, so that no root of
" bitterness should ever spring up again to trouble this por-
" tion of the heritage of God." This report is signed by
Robert Ralston, as President, Isaac Snowden, John White,
and Peter Lesley, as Committee.

It is just here that a little light is thrown upon the apparent causes of the disaffection, by a fragment that has been
preserved. Mr. Sanford was, in some respects, an innovator,
and in others strongly conservative. One of the things
which seemed to give much offence was, that he required
persons who united with the church to rise in their places,
when their names were called, and give public assent to the
articles of faith, as well as to enter into covenant with the
church to walk in the ordinances of God's house blameless.
This was not in accordance with the long-established custom
of introducing members, who were received by the Session,

and their names recorded, but not announced in public. On
the other hand, the custom of distributing tokens to the
communicants on the Saturday evening before the administration of the Lord's Supper, and taking .them up in plates
passed for that purpose while the communicants were seated
at the table, had been discontinued. This custom Mr. Sanford sought to revive, and insisted upon its re-adoption.
These, and perhaps other unessential matters, were magnified,
and became the occasion, though probably not wholly the
cause, of great disaffection and the final disruption. Robert
Ralston, Charles Chauncey, Isaac Snowden, Peter Lesley, and
other eminent men remained with the old church. This
defection was a serious loss. It not only greatly lessened
the numbers and weakened the financial condition of the
church, but some of the best families and most influential
members removed their relation to Cherry street.

The members of the old congregation, however, set their
hands again to the work of restoration and recovery. They
soon called the Rev. Dr. Cornelius C. Cuyler, of the Dutch
Reformed Church, who had been eminently successful as a
preacher and pastor in Poughkeepsie, New York. After his
settlement and adjustment to the work in his new field, the
question of removal to some more central location began to

CHURCH IN SEVENTH STREET:—Built in 1837.

E

be agitated, and after much discussion and some considerable feeling about going so far to the westward, lots were secured on Seventh street, a little below Arch, and on the sixth day of September, 1836, the corner stone of a new church building was laid. On the sixteenth of July of the next year the building was dedicated and opened for divine worship.

We present a view on page 57.

"The front of this building was of marble, and the interior "chaste and commodious. The pulpit was of pure white "marble, built somewhat in the form of a mausoleum. It "rested upon a platform about a foot high. The lower por- "tion of the pulpit was about five feet high and fifteen feet "long, a complete parallelogram. The central portion of "this pulpit, and resting upon the parallelogram, was a piece "of marble, five feet in length, and two feet or more in "height, surmounted by a large and beautiful velvet cushion. "In front of the pulpit stood a communion table of carved "mahogany, covered with a slab of variegated marble, and in "the recess back of the pulpit was a tablet to the memory of "Whitefield and Tennent."

But the removal from the old site, the erection of a new and attractive building, and the settlement of an honored and successful pastor, did not prove an instant success. Too

much of the life-blood of the church had been drawn away.
The new location did not prove to be the best, notwithstanding the high hopes expressed at the laying of the corner
stone.   Causes not anticipated hindered the growth of the
church.   The tide had not only reached their western location, but swept far beyond them.   Families gradually changed
their residence, and frequently removed too far away to be
able to worship longer in the old church.   The older members died, and no younger members took their place.   With
this ceaseless drain, which could neither be stopped nor the
heavy losses supplied, both Dr. Cuyler and his successor, Dr.
Shields, were obliged to struggle and to struggle in vain.
Our venerated and now sainted brother and elder, Dr. Hugh
L. Hodge, says of these times and of the location in Seventh
street : —

"The congregation, having taken possession of their new and beautiful edifice
"in 1836, entertained strong hopes of a revival of their former prosperity, and
"for a time these hopes seemed about to be realized.   The fact, however, became
"soon evident that the new location of our church was most unfortunate.   There
"were two large Presbyterian congregations in our neighborhood, and families
"were gradually deserting this part of the City for more favorable residences
"south and west; hence the accession to our numbers was small, while the
"original membership was gradually diminished by death and removals; hence,
"notwithstanding the excellence and devotion of our pastor, Dr. Cuyler, and the

"subsequent labors of his successor, the talented and eloquent Dr. Shields, now
" Professor in Princeton College, our numbers gradually dwindled, and it became
" evident that this position could not be maintained.   No one saw this more
" clearly, or labored more sedulously to accomplish a removal, than Dr. Shields.
" To him it was a subject of much anxious thought and of repeated conversation
" with leading members of the church ; but the way was not opened, and it was
" not until some years afterwards that, under a sense of the stern necessity of the
" case, and after much discussion, it was determined, in the spring of 1867, to
" sell our church building, and erect another one in a more promising part of
" the City."

At this point begins the history of the movement which resulted in the purchase of the lot and the erection of the church building on the corner of Walnut and Twenty-first streets.   On the resignation of Dr. Shields the present pastor was called, and entered upon his labors in the Autumn of 1865.   The condition of the church was not promising.   But few families remained, and of these many of the children had scattered to other churches, or found a home in other denominations.   The old prestige was gone.   God had evidently said by His providences long before : — "*Arise ye, and depart, " for this is not your rest.*"   It was almost melancholy to see the fragments of these ancient and honored households gathered around the ashes of the fires which their fathers had kindled, and long ago had gone out.

With great effort, upon the part of the few people who
remained, a new interest was awakened, and for a time new
life seemed to be infused. Congregations increased, and the
house was filled. But the new congregations were made up
of transient people, and the church did not greatly add to its
membership. Many of the causes which had wrought so
disastrously against its success were still in force. Its position
was daily becoming more untenable. No human power could
arrest the drift of business or the tide of peoples. It was
impossible to save the church in its old location. Like a
stranded ship, from which the tide had ebbed away, never to
return, nothing could be done for it. After much discussion,
and many meetings for consultation and prayer, it was at last
decided to leave the old ground, which had been occupied for
twenty-eight years, and seek a location in some more western
part of the City. The property was advertised, and sold at
auction.

After the sale, the Horticultural Hall, corner of Broad and
Spruce streets, was secured for public worship on the Sabbath,
the congregation having no home beyond this temporary
sojourn. Early in January, 1868, an invitation was received
from the Fifth Presbyterian Church, in Arch street above
Tenth, not only to worship with them, but to unite the two

bodies under the pastor of the Second .Church.   The propo-
sition went to the Central Presbytery, and the union was
declared to be inexpedient and impossible.

In the meantime there was great diversity of opinion with
regard to a new location.   The old objection of going too far
west was urged against the proposed site at Walnut and
Twenty-first streets.   The time passed on, and nearly a year
was spent in the Horticultural Hall.   But a wandering church
could not prosper any more than a settled one in an out of
the way place.   It became a question of action or dissolution,
and upon the most careful advice, and with most earnest
prayer for the Divine direction, the lot on the corner of
Walnut and Twenty-first streets was purchased.   By this
final action we lost some of the influential and wealthy
members of the church, but the lot secured was in the midst
of a cultivated and rapidly increasing population.   The rem-
nant that was left gathered courage, and having raised a
subscription of thirty-three thousand dollars, broke ground
on the twenty-sixth day of March, 1869.   To furnish a resting place for our weary feet, and a room where we could
gather what was left of our scattered forces while the building
was going up, the plain structure in the rear of this building
was erected, and by courtesy called a chapel.   To this modest

building were transferred a part of the pulpit, the pews, and
the gas fixtures of the church in Seventh street, which gave
it quite a home-like appearance. On the seventh of January,
1869, with tears of gratitude and songs of thanksgiving we
entered that humble place of prayer.

The corner stone of this new building was laid by the
pastor, June 21, 1869. Rev. W. A. Musgrave, D. D., made
the address. On the thirteenth day of October, 1872, it
was dedicated to the worship of Almighty God. Two sermons were preached by the pastor : In the morning, from
Psalm xcvi., 6, — "*Strength and beauty are in His sanctuary ;*"
and in the evening, from Isaiah lvi., 7, — "*My house shall be
"called a house of prayer for all people.*" A week of services
followed, conducted by some of the most eminent ministers
in the land.

The work accomplished by this church since its organization in 1743 cannot now be told. A few facts only can be
stated. It has erected three church buildings. The first
Sabbath school in the City, and perhaps in the country, was
established in its congregation. The Bible Society owes its
early successes, if not its origin, to its ministry and benefactions. It has educated in its parochial school some of the
foremost men and women of Philadelphia. It has gathered a

great army of converts for the Lord Jesus, furnished men for the ministry, and given many members to churches of other denominations.   It has contributed largely in benefactions, cared for many poor widows and orphan children, and made a record of service and fidelity of which neither our fathers nor their descendents need be ashamed.   In the work of building this house our people have done nobly, and are entitled to great credit.   The structure will speak for itself.

The property has largely increased in value, and in turn has added to the value of all estates in its neighborhood.

Permanent benefactions to the church are as follows : —

Pulpit and wing walls, seats around the apsis, and carpet for the pulpit, with the five stained glass windows in the rear : from the late Theodore Cuyler, esq,, in memory of his father, Rev. Cornelius C. Cuyler, D. D.

Baptismal font, of stone, beautifully carved : from the late William Struthers, in memory of his father, John Struthers.

One two-light stained glass window, on the west aisle : from Charles F. Haseltine.

One two-light stained glass window, in the west aisle : from James L. Harmer, to the memory of Mrs. Sarah Coit Lauman Harmer.

One two-light stained glass window, in west aisle: contributed to the memory of James Vanuxem, by Mary Vanuxem Wurts, daughter of the late James Vanuxem.

One two-light stained glass window, in east aisle: from C. E. Claghorn, to the memory of Alice Niles Miller.

One two-light stained glass window, in the east aisle: from the late Miss Rebecca Snowden, to the memory of Isaac Snowden, a former elder in the church.

A single light stained glass window, in the east transept: from Mary Cole, to the memory of James Hunter Cole.

Two one-light windows, in the east transept, from William and Edmund Smith, to the memory of Robert Smith and Robert Hobart Smith, both of whom were formerly elders in this church.

A fund now amounting to twelve thousand six hundred dollars: given by Elias Boudinot in 1812, the interest of which to be expended annually for "poor pious women and "children."

The Spencer Trust, a ground rent which yields $48 per annum: to be used for the poor of the church.

Two silver goblets, for the communion service: presented by Rev. Gilbert Tennent. A silver tankard: presented by John Sproat; and four silver plates, presented by Dr. Hugh L. Hodge.

The Bible which graces our pulpit was presented by Mr. Lemuel Coffin, of Holy Trinity.

A valuable library for the pastor, and teachers of the Sabbath school, and another for the scholars, were presented by a member of our church whose name cannot appear.

A most interesting and valuable collection of biblical illustrations, gathered in part by the pastor, in Palestine, were presented by the late Mrs. Parthenia P. Mayfield.

The actual membership of the church in these generations it is not possible to know with certainty; it must amount to thousands. We reached this ground, after all the depletions by separations and waste of years, with about sixty living members, the larger number women. We now number nearly or quite four hundred.

Our journey is ended. We stand to-day in this beautiful house of prayer, with eye undimmed and force unabated, one hundred and thirty-three years old. With trembling lips, as we tell the story of our birth, our trials, and our victory, we give all praise to God. He led our fathers: He has been a covenant-keeping God with their children and their children's children. Among us still are honored disciples, who remember well the house and the ordering of the service in Arch street. They know all the way in which the Lord has led His people. We give them joy that they have lived to see this church, which their fathers founded, and in which they themselves were born and baptized, rise in beauty and grandeur in this latter day toward the setting sun. They will bear on toward the grave rich memories of the past and a brighter outlook for the time to come.

PRESBYTERIANS owe much to this old Second Church.

In all the generations of her history she has been faithful to the truth. No uncertain sound has been given by the men who blew silver trumpets on her walls. In all contentions and discussions about doctrines, measures, or men, she was mighty for God and the truth. The great men whose names are enrolled upon her records, and whose lives make her history, were heroic defenders of the faith. Their work and their memories have outlived the noisy and discordant strife of tongues. The mystic seed of the kingdom which they sowed, often in tears, has taken root and filled the land.

AMERICA owes much to this ancient church of God.

Her strong men helped to lay the foundations and built on the walls of this Republic. Presbyterian principles, like the old Roman cement, went into the structure of the national government. They were sought in council, and followed as leaders, in the times that tried men's souls.

PHILADELPHIA owes her much.

Identified with all the history of this early colony, and now second city of the republic, she has been from the beginning a tower of strength, a beauty, and a defence. She has trained for places of honor and trust some of Philadelphia's noblest men and women. She planted in the wilderness " the fir tree, "and the pine, and the box together." She has kept pace with the march of improvement and the migrating of peoples. On your western borders she has reared in these last days a home for her children, and a house of prayer for all people. This beautiful house we do not present to you as an evidence of our taste or a monument of our skill. We have built grandly, and for the ages, but we have built for God. As our fathers did before us, we have given to Him the best. Some of us did not expect to worship long in this building, but we built as if we were to remain here alway. No man

of our company wrought more faithfully, prayed more earnestly, or gave more liberally, for the success of this work,
than did that dear old servant of God,* who lived long
enough to pass the threshold, and worship the God of his
fathers in this completed structure, but whose sightless eyes
never saw its beauty. The labor of our hands lies in these
walls. The massive granite and stately columns hold our
confession of faith. The record of the agonies, the strong
crying and tears, the sore travail, the wrestling with God,
is on high.

Mother of churches, and mother of mighty men! She has
renewed her youth. She has put on her beautiful garments,
and is adorned as a bride for the Lamb. Her children are
gathered again by her side, and in the household there is
thanksgiving and joy. Bless her, ye that dwell in her courts,
and ye that pass by, for Jehovah hath blessed her, and she
shall be blessed for evermore.

---

* Dr. Hugh L. Hodge.

III.

Eph. iv.: 11, 12.

" And He gave some, apostles; and some, prophets; and some, evangelists; and " some, pastors and teachers: For the perfecting of the saints, for the work of " the ministry, for the edifying of the body of Christ."

NATIONS must have rulers; armies, leaders; all effective organizations, a head. God has planted the human race upon the earth, to work out the problems of life and probation: — "the earth hath he given "to the children of men," and upon it he has set them in families like a flock. For safety, defence, better training, to answer the social and gregarious instincts of human nature, they gather into cities, villages, communities, and these must have government, order, law; and so rulers, chiefs, or head-men, what Carlyle calls able men. The church is but the family enlarged, a community which must have order, help, government, as well as the State. No church can be complete in its organization, or equipped for its proper work without an overseer, leader, guide. The beautiful name given in the scriptures is pastor, or shepherd. Christ is the Great Shepherd who watches over the flock, — the Church of God. Pastors are the under-shepherds, placed over individual flocks, who are to care for those committed to their keeping, as a shepherd cares for his sheep. They are to feed them, fold them, lead them into green pastures, and defend them even with life.

This divine arrangement is for the "*perfecting of the saints,* "*the work of the ministry, and the edifying of the body of* "*Christ.*" The great end is that the church may be trained ; everything well ordered and appointed, that Christians may have the best possible means of instruction, all healthful advantages to increase in knowledge, grow in grace, and be built up in the most holy faith. The church which He has bought with His blood is Christ's special care in this world. As it was expedient for Him to go away when His work on earth was done, He has left the work of Christian training in the hands of men whom He calls and ordains to this service, — some, apostles ; some, prophets ; some, evangelists ; and some, pastors and teachers : various offices,

suited to the times and needs of the church, and all to minister to the same end, the "edifying of the body of Christ."
The church is to be built, — built up, — foundations laid,
walls go up, topmost stone put in place, and for this there
must be workmen, wise master builders, apt to teach, faithful
to guide, and who need not be ashamed.

These officers are Christ's gift to His Church. He calls
men, trains them by His providence, gives them His Spirit,
endows them with gifts, sets them over His flock, and makes
them responsible for the safety of every soul committed to
their care. We have passed rapidly over the external history
of the Second Church, the gathering of its congregations,
erection of its buildings, the going out of its people, from
time to time, to establish new centres and occupy new fields.
It is impossible to complete and round the history of this old
and honored church of Christ without studying the men
whose hands laid her foundations and built on her walls.
Their lives made her history ; their names are inwrought in
every record that has come down to us ; they gathered the
people, and led them as a shepherd does his flock. Their
illustrious names and heroic deeds gave power to her counsels
and grandeur to her achievements, and the memory of their
noble examples and successful work are our richest inheri-

F

tance. We are not to garnish their sepulchres, but to perpetuate their memories, live again their lives, carry on their
masterly work. The fathers shall teach us, shall live again
in their children and in their children's children.

GEORGE WHITEFIELD was the founder of this church, but
never a pastor. In the strictest sense, he was an evangelist.
After his ordination by Bishop Bevan, in Gloucester, England,
it may be said that he went everywhere preaching the word.
Dr. Sprague classes him among the Episcopalians. As he
associated much with the Wesleys, and preached like them in
the fields, the English people classed him with the Methodists. As he preached in America, where Presbyterians were
numerous, and gathered Presbyterian churches, he passed
among us for a good Presbyterian. He is neither one of
these now.

In a curious pamphlet which was published in London, and
reprinted and sold by William Bradford in 1749, in Second
street, Whitefield answers the charges made against the Methodists, in a scurrilous publication, apparently by a clergyman of
the Church of England. One charge was : — "That after the
" Methodists had traduced the clergy as long as they were
" permitted to do it, in their own churches and pulpits, they
" set about this pious work of defamation more heartily in

"the fields." To this Whitefield replies : — " On such a day,
" the Rev. Mr. Whitefield, after having had an University
" education, been regularly ordained deacon and priest of the
" Church of England, and invited to preach in most churches
" of the cities of Gloucester, Bristol, Westminster, and London
" (in the last of which places he collected near a thousand
" pounds sterling for the charity children), being causelessly
" denied the further use of the churches, because he preached
" the necessity of the new birth, and justification in the sight
" of God by faith alone in the imputed righteousness of Jesus
" Christ, began to preach the same doctrines in the fields."

Novelty was another charge : — " But though this danger-
" ous and presumptious sect, strolling predicants, itinerant
" enthusiasts, have allured some itching ears, and drawn them
" aside by calumniating their proper pastors, they have sense
" enough to know the itch will go off, and their trade not
" continue long, unless they can produce something novel or
" uncommon, what the wandering sheep have not been used
" to in their churches." His manly answer to novelty in
doctrines is this : —" The doctrines we chiefly insist upon
" are these : — That man is very far gone from original right-
" eousness : that he cannot turn and prepare himself by his
" own natural strength and good works to faith and calling

"upon God: that we are accounted righteous before God
"only for the merit of our Lord and Saviour Jesus Christ,
"by faith, and not for our own works or deserving: that
"albeit good works are fruits of faith, and follow after justifi-
"cation, cannot put away our sins, and endure the severity
"of God's judgment, yet are they pleasing and acceptable
"to God in Christ, and do spring out necessarily of a true
"and lively faith; insomuch that by them a lively faith may
"be evidently known, as a tree is discerned by its fruits."

The great battle was over these doctrines. His first sermon
in London was in Bishopsgate Church, August 4, 1737. As he
went up the pulpit stairs the people sneered at him on account
of his youth, but they grew serious in the time of preaching,
and showed great respect as he passed down. Soon after he
preached in Bow Church, Cheapside, which was exceedingly
crowded, and for nearly three months after preached from
church to church to immense throngs. Constables were
placed without and within. Thousands went away from the
largest churches for want of room. On Sunday mornings,
long before day, the streets were filled with people going to
church, with their lanterns in their hands, and conversing
about the things of God.

All this produced great excitement, and awakened strong

opposition. Many sermons were preached against him; letters and pamphlets published; and to oppose Whitefield was a means of preferment at court. Bishops, curates, and chaplains made him the target of their keenest shafts. But the young hero continued to preach, to the immense throngs, who hurried to and fro wherever he was announced, the necessity of the new birth and the old doctrine of justification by faith. The opposition became so fierce at last that churches, one after another, were closed against him. He then resorted to the fields, and throngs followed him to Moorfields and Blackheath. He preached in churchyards and from stone walls, sometimes the mob threatening his life, and men lying in wait for him.

In this same spirit, and preaching these same doctrines, he came to America and landed at Philadelphia. Churches here were few, and these for the most part were closed against him, but God's heavens were over him, and streets and fields were accessible. In the balcony of the old Court House in Second street, and on the steps, and on Society Hill, by the flagstaff, he invaded the religious formalism of the time by thundering the doctrines of the reformation. At the sound of his voice the people ran together, and listened with great eagerness. As in London, under his preaching the attention of the people

was greatly drawn to eternal things. Great awakening followed. The work spread: the whole City was moved. A
great change passed over the society of Philadelphia. All
classes became serious and thoughtful, earnest, and many
were converted to God.

From these converts one hundred and forty were gathered,
after careful selection and examination, and formed into a
church. It was called the Second Presbyterian Church in
Philadelphia, as the First was already in existence, and had a
house on High street, below Third. The formation of this
church was the culmination of Whitefield's work in Philadelphia. He gathered the sheep into the fold, and then went
on his way to search for the lost in regions beyond. He
commenced preaching at twenty-two years of age, and finished at fifty-six, having preached eighteen thousand times,
an average of more than ten times a week for thirty-four
years. Probably no man ever lived on the earth who preached
Christ to so many people, or gathered so many souls for the
King of Glory. His last sermon was preached at Exeter, in
the open air, to a great multitude, on Saturday, September 29,
1770. He went on to Newburyport the same evening, where
he was to preach on the morrow. Wearied and worn he
went to his bed, and slept till two the next morning, when he

awoke, oppressed for breath. At five, sitting in his chair, with no words but these, " I am dying," he finished his work, and went to his reward. By such a man, in such a spirit, and from the fruits of such a work, was the Second Church founded.

The revival influences continued for a long time, and the work was taken up by other hands. The infant church was made up of the best materials that could be gathered into its organization, but needed at once some master-hand to give shape and direction to its energies and life.

Attention was turned to GILBERT TENNENT, and he was called. He was born in the county of Armagh, in Ireland, in 1703, and came with his father to America when fourteen years of age. He studied with his father, received a degree from Yale in 1725, and was ordained by the Presbytery of Philadelphia in 1726. He was settled at New Brunswick, and his preaching excited great attention from the very commence- ment of his ministry. His fame reached to England and Scotland.

Nillison, of Dundee, says : —

" In the year 1740, Mr. Whitefield went to New England, " and Mr. Gilbert Tennent after him, where they preached two " or three times a day with singular and extraordinary suc-

" cess, the people being greatly awakened, especially by Mr.
" Tennent's preaching, so that there followed a remarkable
" change upon their lives, and a wonderful revival and appear-
" ance of religion through all that country for several years.
" The like also was very observable in Pennsylvania and the
" Jerseys about the same time."

This, doubtless, was a distant echo of that celebrated preaching tour in New England in 1740, and the great work in
Philadelphia.   Tennent reached Boston December 13th, and
preached to great crowds almost daily for three months.   The
results were indeed extraordinary.   Mr. Prince, the minister of
the Old South Church, describes his manner as "both terrible
" and searching.   By his rousing and spiritual preaching deep
" and pungent convictions were wrought in the minds of many
" hundreds in the town, and the same effect was produced in
" several scores in the neighboring congregations.   And now
" was such a time as we never knew.   The Rev. Mr. Cooper
" said that more came to him in one week in deep concern
" than in the whole twenty-four years of his preceding min-
" istry.   I can say also the same as to the numbers who
" repaired to me."

Such was the man called to the first pastorate of the Second
Church, after sixteen years of experience as preacher and

pastor. He commenced his work in May, 1743. He somewhat calmed down in these days, and lamented his "extrava-
"gancy in discarding a wig, and in wearing his hair loose
"and unpowdered, with a great coat belted with a leathern
"belt, during his preaching tour in New England."

"It is related, that in 1747 a French privateer came into
"Delaware Bay. The citizens of Philadelphia met in the new
"meeting-house, and formed an association for defence. Ten-
"nent preached to them from Exodus xv.: 3 : — ' *The Lord*
" ' *is a man of war.*' "

When the British army entered Philadelphia in 1778, it was
greatly in want of paper for cartridges, and only after a long
search could any be obtained. At last there were found, in
the garret of a house where Benjamin Franklin previously
had his printing office, twenty-five hundred copies of this
sermon on "Defensive War," which had been printed by
Franklin. These were all taken, and speedily used to wrap
cartridges, which won the battle of Monmouth.

The first house occupied by the Second Church was the
"large brick building" built by the multitude for Whitefield,
and for the "use of itinerant preachers forever." In 1750,
this building was sold for an Academy, which in 1779 became the University of Pennsylvania.

The congregation soon procured a site at Third and Arch streets, and Tennent set himself to the work of erecting a new house for the worship of God. He went to Franklin, to ask whom he should call upon for help. Franklin told him to call on everybody. With unceasing energy he prosecuted the work, and at the end of two years the congregation entered the new structure.

A note says : —

" The new Presbyterian church in Philadelphia, a large, " elegant, and stately fabric, owes its erection to the inde- " fatigable industry of Gilbert Tennent, by which he procured " the greatest part of the money in benefactions, though the " house cost some thousands."

At the dedication two sermons were preached by the pastor, in which he says : —

" Divine Providence has appeared surprisingly in the course " and series of these transactions. We were brought at first " under a sudden, unexpected, and urgent necessity of en- " deavoring to get a house for ourselves to worship God in, " the issue of which, because of the difficulty of the enterprise, " and the low state of the generality of your society, appeared " not only very doubtful and precarious, but, without assis-

"tance from others, entirely impossible. This, of course, af-
"fected the minds of some with fear and solicitude for the
"event.   But it has pleased a gracious God to dissipate our
"fears, and to turn that which seemed to threaten our dissolu-
"tion into the probable means of establishing the society for
"a long time to come.   The glorious sovereignty of the
"Divine Providence is seen in fixing the place where the
"church now stands; a situation in respect to free air in the
"Summer, warmth in the Winter, and open prospect, is perhaps
"not inferior to any in the City.   A kind Providence has
"mercifully appeared in inclining the hearts of a considerable
"number of our own people to contribute generously to erect
"a house for God; and Divine Providence has been still more
"conspicuous in inclining many worthy gentlemen of other
"societies to befriend and assist us with their generous dona-
"tions; and I do gladly embrace this public opportunity, to
"thank in the most respectful manner, in the name and behalf
"of this Society, His Honor the Governor, The Honorable
"the Chief Justice, the Secretary of this Province, and The
"Worshipful the Mayor and Recorder of this City, and all
"the Honorable Gentlemen of the Council and Assembly, and
"of every other station and character in life, who have con
"tributed to the building of this church."

For twenty years this faithful servant of God labored for
this church, and his whole ministry was marked with striking
diligence and success.   On the 23rd of July, 1764, he died.

Dr. Finley, in his funeral sermon, says of him : —

"As to his person, he was taller than the common size, and
"every way proportionable.   His aspect was grave and ven-
"erable, but he was eminently affable, condescending, and
"communicative.   He was of a truly public spirit, and warmly
"interested himself in whatever seemed to contribute to the
"safety and advantage of the Province.   He was an example
"of great fortitude and unshaken resolution.   Difficulties
"were so far from dispiriting, that they rather animated him
"in his efforts.   A great part of his life was a scene of un-
"remitted labor.   He studied hard, traveled much, and
"preached often.   As a preacher, few equaled him in his
"vigorous days.   His reasoning powers were strong; his
"thoughts nervous, and often sublime ; his style, flowery and
"diffusive ; his manner of address, warm and pathetic, such
"as must convince his audience that he was in earnest, and
"his voice clear and commanding.   In a word, all things
"conspired to make him a judicious, zealous, popular, and
"pungent preacher."

JOHN MURRAY was called as the second pastor. He remained but a single year. He afterwards settled in Newburyport, in Massachusetts, where he established a reputation as
an able and devoted minister. A vacancy of three years followed, when Rev. James Sproat was called as the third pastor.

JAMES SPROAT was born in Scituate, Massachusetts, in 1722.
His father died when he was young, and he was left in charge
of a small farm, in company with an Indian named Tom Felix,
to whom he was strongly attached. At thirteen, his widowed
mother proposed he should try to get an education, and fit
himself for usefulness. After many struggles, the greatest
of which seemed to be the separation from his Indian companion and friend, he entered Yale. He was young and gay,
and found new companions in college, who were much like
himself, and in the society of these new friends he soon lost
the impressions which his pious mother's instructions had
made upon his mind. About this time Gilbert Tennent made
his tour through New England, and stopped at New Haven.
His fame as one of the "new light" preachers had reached
Yale College. Before his coming, the class to which young
Sproat belonged arranged a plan for brow-beating Tennent,
by placing him in a ridiculous light. They dressed themselves very gaily, and went into the front of the gallery,

directly opposite to the preacher, and all stood, looking directly at him.   The text was Matthew v. : 20 : — "*Except* "*your righteousness shall exceed the righteousness of the scribes* "*and pharisees, ye shall in no wise enter into the kingdom of* "*heaven.*"   In explaining the passage, he gave an interesting account of the scribes and pharisees, and then, addressing his hearers, he said with peculiar emphasis : — " If *your* right- " eousness does not exceed theirs you will *be damned,*" striking the pulpit violently as he pronounced the word "damned." The word, the manner in which it was pronounced, the vehemence of gesture which accompanied it, had such an effect upon Sproat and several others of the class that they sat down, and did not lift their heads during the remainder of the sermon.   When Sproat returned to the college from the meeting, he went to his room, locked the door, and in great distress threw himself upon the floor.   His distress continued through the night, and the next day he went to see and converse with Mr. Tennent.   When he came to the house where he lodged, he walked three or four times around it before he could persuade himself to enter.   At length he went in, and ventured to make known his distress.   Mr. Tennent received him kindly, and earnestly presented the way of salvation through Christ.

This account, which I find in an old manuscript, which seems to have been written many years afterwards, ends with these words : — " So Sproat himself became one of the ' new "' lights,' although he had despised them so much before."

He graduated in 1741, and went at once to Northampton to study theology with Mr. Edwards, boarding with a French family, by whom he was instructed in the French language. He first preached in Albany, New York, and from there went into Connecticut, and in the first town where he preached he was arrested as a vagrant, for preaching in that colony without permission from the minister of the parish. He was handed from constable to constable until he reached Saybrook. The constable there was a " new light," and when he understood that young Sproat had been apprehended as a " new light " minister, he dismissed him, telling him he might go where he pleased. He went to Guilford, where he was favorably received by a number of the inhabitants, who formed themselves into a church, and called him to be their minister. They built a meeting-house for him, and he was ordained and settled August 23, 1743. In this church he labored for twenty-five years with eminent zeal and success.

From Guilford he was called to Philadelphia, and March 30th, 1769, was installed pastor of the Second Presbyterian

Church. Under his ministry the church prospered, and passed
safely through the trying vicissitudes incident to the war and
the occupation of the City by the British. Some notices of
his preaching and work were made by John Adams, who was
attending the meetings of Congress in Philadelphia, and became the second President of the United States.

September 4th, 1774, Mr. Adams says : — "Went to the
" Presbyterian meeting, and heard Mr. Sproat, in the forenoon.
" He uses no notes, opens his bible, and talks away." On the
eleventh (the following Sabbath) : — "Mr. Jo. Reed, a very
" sensible and accomplished lawyer, was so kind as to wait
" on us to Mr. Sproat's meeting. We had an opportunity of
" seeing the custom of the Presbyterians in administering the
" sacrament. The communicants all came to a row of seats
" placed on each side of a narrow table, spread in the middle
" of the alley, reaching from the deacon's seat to the front
" of the house. Each communicant has a token, which he
" delivers to the deacons."

September 17th, 1775 : — "Heard Sproat on Titus iii. : 5.
" There is a great deal of simplicity and innocence in this
" worthy man, but very little eloquence or ingenuity. In
" prayer he hangs his head in an angle of forty-five degrees
" over his left shoulder. In sermon, which is delivered without

"notes, he throws himself into a variety of postures. He
"has no imagination, no passions, but a great deal of good-
"ness of heart."

Two years later, Mr. Adams thought enough of this good
man and minister to go to his house to board. September
12, 1777:—"I removed from Captain Duncan's in Walnut
"street, to the Rev. Mr. Sproat's, in Third street, a few doors
"from his meeting house. Mr. Marchant, of Rhode Island,
"boards there with me. Mr. Sproat is sick of a fever. Mrs.
"Sproat and the four young ladies, his daughters, are in great
"distress on account of his sickness and the approach of
"Howe's army." Howe's army was then at Middletown, in
Lancaster county, waiting for his ships to come into the
Delaware. Soon after, Congress was obliged to fly from
Philadelphia, and John Adams and his good friend were
separated.

In 1793, Philadelphia suffered from the terrible scourges of
the yellow fever. It raged in its most malignant form, and
the mortality was appalling. Fear was on every side, and the
panic so great, that the dead were hurried to the grave in
hearses and carts without attendants. But this noble man
and faithful minister stood at his post. A thousand fell at his
side, his neighbors and friends were stricken down, and at

G

length the pestilence crossed his own threshold. Within a month his eldest son, his son's wife, and his youngest daughter, died.

In a letter to an absent son he says : —

" Dear John : — Your poor old trembling father must be " the sorrowful messenger of grief upon grief to you. Your " brother William is no more. I shall attend his remains to " the grave at six o'clock. Maria knows not of her husband's " death. Your mother, exceedingly feeble, has not been able " to see her son. We are all dying in the City."

The son's wife soon followed; and a little later, the feeble mother and the poor old trembling father, were both laid in the grave. Amid these distressing scenes, it was touching to see the respect shown to the memory of this eminent servant of God. Some religious negroes voluntarily offered to carry the bier to the grave. The pious people who met at the church for prayer found a procession of about fifty persons, and " this was more startling to the beholders, in the circum- " stances in which it happened, than the most splendid funeral " that perhaps the City ever witnessed."

Mr. Thomas Bradford says : —

" I remember Dr. Sproat as a venerable looking man. (Dr.
" Sproat received the degree of Doctor of Divinity from the
" College of New Jersey in 1780.) He always wore the wig
" and the cocked hat, according to the usage of aged ministers
" of that period. He possessed a benevolent countenance; his
" manners were gentle and courteous ; his speech conciliating
" and kind, especially toward the youthful part of his flock,
" who were attracted to him by his paternal and affectionate
" treatment of them."

Dr. Ashbel Green, who was for a time a co-pastor, and who
succeeded him in the pastorate of the church, says : —

" On all occasions he treated me like a father, and like a
" father I loved and honored him. In scholastic attainments
" he was a good proficient, and a considerable master of the
" learned languages. He loved all the pursuits and interests
" of science, and in the study of divinity made a progress that
" was truly great and enviable. In his personal religion he
" was truly eminent, and after his fiftieth year in the ministry
" he spent much time in private devotion. In his sore domes-
" tic afflictions his Christian fortitude and trust were remark-
" able. Trembling with age, and with the fearful disease

" which was to end his life already upon him, he followed his
" dead son to the grave, and leaning upon his staff, as he
" looked upon the body lying at rest, he said : — " The Lord
" gave, and the Lord hath taken away ; blessed be the name
" of the Lord." As he drew near himself to die, he said : —
" All my expectations for eternity rest on the infinite grace of
" God, abounding through the finished righteousness of our
" Lord Jesus."

Such men laid the foundations of the Second Church, and
each built in his time on the chief corner-stone. They were
men of most pronounced character and undoubted success.
Master-workmen, who did not build of hay, wood, and
stubble, or daub with untempered mortar. The doctrines of
the reformation were preached with great fidelity and power,
and God gave the increase. The small beginning grew till it
became a tree which shadowed the land. And when these
servants of God had finished their work, and slept with their
fathers, God raised up others to take their place, and the
succession never has been broken.

IV.

***

John iv.: 37, 38.

***

" And herein is that saying true, One soweth, and another reapeth. I sent
" you to reap that whereon ye bestowed no labor : other men labored, and ye are
" entered into their labors."

***

ALL men are workers. Labor is the law, and toil the duty, of human life. Every man has something to do in this world, and will have both post and service assigned. He must serve his generation, then fall on sleep, and his work pass to other hands. No workers could ask for better conditions, or more helpful appliances, or greater rewards, than belong to honest labor and lawful callings on this earth.

So there is a proper distribution and apportionment. Laborers in every field, suited for every service, and provided for every age. One generation passeth away, and another cometh, and yet each, in its own time, has its own proper work to do. There is a succession of laborers, as times, and seasons, and centuries come and go. One soweth, and another reapeth. One man plants a tree, and another eats the fruit thereof. No one man can do all, and no generation live to enjoy wholly the fruit of its own labors. We build for others to inhabit ; make highways over which the nations who are to come after us, are to pass. We do the work, and build the structures which are needful for our time, and suited to present necessities, or the state of human knowledge ; but we complete nothing. We take up the work where others left it, and others, in turn, will lift the burden which we lay down.

In the Egyptian quarries we find the tools of the workmen that were used under Pharoah's task-masters, and after lying idle for four thousand years, other hands take them up. Not wholly suited to our time and need; but they embody the thought of the ancient time, and have survived to show how the ages are linked together, and the works of men pass from hand to hand, and improve from age to age.

Ages have been sowing seed. The good which men do, and the evil, live after them. So relays of toilers, strength of burden-bearers and brain workers decays, and they must be

relieved. Nearly three generations of men wrought on the
Cathedral at Cadiz, in Spain. The Duomo at Cologne is not yet
finished, though the foundations were laid more than six hundred years ago. The Minster, at York, has the old Saxon
crypts that were built a thousand years ago.

Works begun by their projectors are rarely finished. Dis-
coveries made by one man are unfolded or applied by another.
Principles are suggested or evolved in one generation, which
take practical form and use in the next. Inventions are announced and put to use; others study them, improve upon
the suggestions, make new applications, and adapt to uses of
which the original inventor had no thought. So of our intellectual wealth. Our libraries are garners where the harvests
of six thousand years are stored. Cities are built by succes-
sive generations. Churches grow, families spread, and become
great, as the ages pass.

Men like Gilbert Tennent, John Murray, and James Sproat,
succeed each other on the same field, each entering into the
labors of those who went before, and leaving the field when
his own work was done, to be cultivated and reaped by those
who should come after him.

Forty-six years of the history of the Second Church had
passed when James Sproat died, and ASHBEL GREEN succeeded

to the pastorate. He was born at Hanover, New Jersey, in 1762, graduated at the College of New Jersey, in 1783. He was the valedictorian of his class, and had the honor of an address to the Father of his Country, George Washington, for which he received the personal thanks of the first President, and was soon after invited to dine with Congress, then sitting at Princeton.

On graduating, at nineteen, Mr. Green was chosen Tutor, and two years later, Professor of Mathematics and Natural Philosophy. In 1787 he became the colleague of Dr. Sproat, and received, from the University of Pennsylvania, the degree of Doctor of Divinity.

With a vigorous intellect, thoroughly trained, eloquent in speech, and masterly in debate, Dr. Green took a prominent part in the ecclesiastical assemblages of the church, where his influence was profoundly great. If he did not originate measures of the first importance, he had an important share in their introduction and settlement. He was a Presbyterian at heart, and his entire life was most closely identified with the local and general interests of the church of his faith and love. Trained in her best schools, and under a man like Witherspoon, with a natural firmness and prompt decision of character, he soon made his way to leadership, and compelled profound respect from both friends and enemies. While officiating as Chaplain to the Senate in session at Philadelphia, the Speaker called the House to order for prayer. A Senator continued writing at his desk. Dr. Green stood silent until the irreverent Senator, startled by the prolonged silence, rose to his feet, and gave at least an outward respect to the worship of God.

Dr. Green's influence was felt in the National Councils. President Adams, who had enjoyed the ministry of Dr. Sproat, and found a home in his family, was drawn also to Dr. Green. On an imminent occasion he requested Dr. Green to write for him a proclamation recommending to the people the observance of a day of humiliation and prayer. The proclamation was written, and embodied the leading doctrines of the gospel. It passed through the hands of Timothy Pickering, who was then Secretary or State, and believed to be a Unitarian; but it was published without alteration, creating great surprise and admiration.

Dr. Green was eminent for his personal piety. The first Monday of every month was observed as a day of fasting, humiliation, and prayer. Three times a day he retired regularly for private devotion. Every Monday morning his brethren in the ministry were invited to meet at his house for reading the Scriptures, and united prayer. His simple and fervent piety made him faithful to all trusts, and punctual in all engagements. He was scrupulously careful in pecuniary transactions. In his charities he acted from principle, not impulse. One-tenth of his income he gave to the Lord, and when occasion seemed to require, he added largely to this tithe.

In October, 1803, he was unanimously elected by the Trustees of the College of New Jersey, to a Professorship of Theology in that Institution; but he chose to remain with his church, in Philadelphia.

As a preacher, Dr. Green took high rank. He loved the pulpit, and says, in one of his letters to his colleague : —

"There is no employment in this world that I love half as "well as preaching. For this I left an honorable literary "establishment at Princeton, when I went to Philadelphia ; "for this I have refused some flattering offers of a similar kind "since ; and for this, I would, I think, cheerfully refuse every "offer to the end of life, that would detach me from it, and "from the people whom I love."

This love for the pulpit and preaching, combined with his large intellectual endowments, his ardent piety, and his rich Christian experience, qualified him in an eminent degree to be a useful public teacher. He wrote his sermons with great care, and "made them at once doctrinal, practical, and experimental."

Dr. Samuel Miller writes of him : —

"I had, when a student in the University, much opportu-
"nity of enjoying his ministry. He was eminently popular.
"No ministers in the City approached him in this respect.
"Crowds flocked to hear him — more than the place of wor-
"ship could contain. His evening services, specially, were
"attended by all denominations; and that not once, or a few
"times only, but from one year's end to another, and for a
"course of years, with unabating interest. And truly his
"discourses were so rich in weighty thought, so beautiful in
"their language, and so powerful in delivery, that they were
"well adapted to gratify all hearers of intelligence and of
"pious taste."

As a *pastor*, he was earnest and faithful. The young he instructed at stated times in the shorter catechism, and his
volumes of lectures on that inimitable synopsis of Christian
faith, are among the classics of the Church. As he was able,
he visited the people at their homes; but as he grew more
infirm with increasing years, he was obliged to forego this
pleasure and duty.

In 1812 Dr. Green was called to the Presidency of the College of New Jersey. After the most earnest deliberation, and under the advice of most trusted friends, he accepted the appointment. He remained in this service for ten years, when his health becoming more infirm, he resigned his position, and returned to Philadelphia.

In this City of his early labors and greatest successes, he spent the remainder of his life preaching the gospel to the poor, preparing his works for the press, and editing the *Christian Advocate*, a periodical which did eminent service for the cause of truth and the Church of God. He lived till 1848, and while the General Assembly was in session at Baltimore, he peacefully closed his life on earth, and entered into rest. His death was announced to that body by Rev. Dr. Cuyler, then pastor of the Second Church, and a large committee was appointed to prepare a suitable minute in regard to his death. He was for twenty-eight years the pastor of this church, and died at the advanced age of eighty-six.

In 1794, Rev. JOHN N. ABEEL, was called as colleague with Dr. Green. He was a pupil, both before, and after, entering college, and Dr. Green had formed a strong attachment for him. After two years, Mr. Abeel received a call to a Reformed

Dutch Church in New York City, which he accepted, and his connection with the Second Church was dissolved. Though the time of his service was short, yet during his stay, Mr. Abeel took an important part of the work. He was eminent as a minister, and faithful as a pastor. Possessed of fine talents, highly cultivated, with extraordinary colloquial gifts, he was everywhere welcomed, both as pastor and friend. By untiring study, and the most diligent application, he gathered large stores of knowledge, which he made greatly useful, both in public labors and social intercourse. His style was plain and simple, but his sermons were profound and effective. He delighted to dwell on " Christian experience, in which he was "always animated and interesting, rising often to uncommon " elegance of diction, and to true eloquence."

He suffered much from ill-health, and visited South Carolina and Brazil, with hope of benefit, if not entire restoration. He continued to fail, however, and returned to New York, where he died in 1812.

Dr. JACOB JONES JANEWAY, was installed the sixth pastor of this church, in 1799. Born in the City of New York, in 1744, he was surrounded by the highest religious influences from his earliest youth. It was the hope of an eminently pious mother that her son should enter the ministry.

During his college course his mind was strongly inclined to the medical profession, but before graduating, having been much exercised on religious subjects, and after a day of fasting and prayer, he decided upon the great life work, to which, from that time, he devoted himself with untiring energy and zeal.

In November, 1797, he was licensed by the Classis of New York, and was soon called to the co-pastorate with Dr. Green, who was then in the very height of his popularity and intellectual strength. Philadelphia was, at that time, the foremost city of the land; one third larger in population than New York, with an immense trade with India and China. The Second Church was, at this time, in its strength, eminent for the character of its ministers, and scarcely less so for the remarkable men of its eldership. It was the generation of Latimer, Jordan, Smith, Henry, Ralston, and others like them. It was with such men, and such a pastor, that young Janeway came at three and twenty to take his place. Without experience in pastoral work; without trial as a preacher, he was to enter upon his duties in a congregation of intelligent and learned men, and make his way to the hearts of his people, and to usefulness in the City. It is something to say, for this youthful preacher, that with such a beginning,

and such a work before him, he held his position with growing influence and power, for nearly thirty years.

To this servant of God, we are largely indebted for the
formation of the Bible Society, which has grown into such a
power, and extended its influence over the world.   In 1808,
associated with Dr. Green, Robert Ralston, and Dr. Benjamin
Rush, a call was issued for a meeting, a constitution prepared,
— which was subsequently adopted — and this work fully
organized and set forward.   Dr. Janeway did much also for
the inauguration of the Foreign Mission work.   It was from
Philadelphia, that Gordon Hall, Samuel Nott, and Luther
Rice embarked for Hindoostan, as the first missionaries to a
foreign field from the American church.   He records the sail-
ing of the ship, and his gratitude to God for the liberal con-
tributions made by the Philadelphia churches to supply the
wants of the missionary company.   He was much interested
in the work of Harriet Newell, and made a large donation
for the work in which she was engaged.   In 1814, he received an urgent call to New Brunswick, which he declined ;
but fourteen years later he accepted the appointment of a
professorship in the Theological Seminary, at Alleghany.
He remained there but two years, however, and then removed to New Brunswick, where he settled over the First

Reformed Dutch Church. With this church he remained until his work on earth was finished.

On Sabbath, June 27, 1857, just before the setting of the sun, he died.

Dr. Janeway was a man of simple and unostentatious manners and habits. Modest and reserved, he never made himself prominent on public occasions, or forced himself into the chief seats. The church heaped honors upon him, but he was as if he knew it not. He was remarkable for purity of life and conversation. Genial and kind to all, he sought only the comfort and well-being of those about him. Gentleness was the law of his heart and his life. He was a life-long student. He sought for truth, and rejoiced as one who had taken spoil, when he found it. Logical, rather than imaginative, with uncommon reasoning powers, his words had great force. Eminent for deliberation and sound judgment, he was a wise counsellor, and his advice was usually followed. The theology of the Bible was his special delight. He was not ashamed to walk in the old paths, or follow where the mighty had trodden before him. Speculations and Broad-Church novelties had no charms for him. He was a Calvinist in the best sense. The sovereignty of God was the great central truth around which his studies and his preaching re-

volved, and the highest joy of his own life. He was a la-
borious man, and fulfilled the inspired words to the letter : —
" *They shall still bring forth fruit in old age.*" At "fourscore
" he was publishing freshly written books." As a preacher,
he was remarkable for sound common sense and clear exhib-
itions of truth, and must have been popular to sustain himself so long, in a large congregation "more frequented by
"strangers than any other in the City." His life was an
important factor in the history of the Second Church, and
exerted a powerful influence upon the City in which he labored so long.

In April, 1813, THOMAS HARVEY SKINNER, was called to
the Second Church, as co-pastor with Dr. Janeway, and remained until the autumn of 1816. He was born in Perquini-
ous County, North Carolina, in 1791. He entered junior at
Princeton, in 1807, and graduated with the second honor at
eighteen. . He at once commenced the study of law, but soon
meeting with an entire change in his religious views, he made
up his mind to obtain a theological education and enter the
Presbyterian ministry. For this purpose he came to Philadelphia, in 1811, to place himself under the care and training of
Dr. Green, but Dr. Green was burdened with too many duties
to assume such a charge, and advised Princeton or Andover.

H

In December, 1812, he was licensed by the Presbytery, at Morristown, N. J., and on the same evening preached his first sermon at Newark. Soon after, he left to return to the South, and passed the last Sabbath in the year in Philadelphia. He preached in the Tabernacle in Ranstead court. Dr. Prentiss says that his name had already become known ; and after the sermon he was waited upon by representatives of the powerful Second Church, Arch street, corner of Third, who urged him to preach for them the next Sabbath. He consented to do so, and this was his first introduction to the congregation of which he was soon to become a pastor. "After preaching "for several weeks, he resumed his journey to the South. "He visited Washington, where his 'eloquent and faithful "'preaching left a deep and most salutary impression.'"

After visiting his friends in North Carolina he returned to Philadelphia, and was ordained as co-pastor, June tenth, 1813. The position was a most trying one. Not only was he to be associated with a man of uncommon power and influence, but at this time there were great diversities of feeling in the churches and community. The "whole atmosphere was "filled with suspicion." There were sharp debates, fierce contentions, and ceaseless strife over doctrines and usages. Excitement ran high, and into the swift current the youthful

athlete threw himself at once, and soon found himself the
leader of a party.   Dr. Green, then President of Nassau
Hall, the senior pastor, and many of the influential members
of his own Church, were opposed to him.   He became a
militant pastor.   Earnest, ardent, full of zeal for his adopted
cause, impatient of restraint, and restive under opposition, his
position could not be otherwise than uncomfortable.

After battling in the very thickest of the conflict for three
years and four months, he resigned his place, and retired,
with some families who were strongly attached to him, to the
building in Locust street, where he was installed in December,
1816.

Fifty years later Dr. Skinner writes of this, his first pastorate, in Philadelphia : —

" A retrospect of my ministry in the Second Presbyterian
" Church, from my present stand-point in time, convinces me
" of uncommon imperfection in it from first to last.   I fear I
" was in rash haste to undertake it.   But two years and four
" months had passed from the date of my conversion ; I was
" in the early part of my twenty-second year ; the church
" was among the first, if not the first, of all the Presbyterian
" order ; my predecessor was a patriarch and ruler in it of

"high distinction. My accepting the call was a great ven-
"ture, and that the result was not my ruin, was of the amaz-
"ing grace of God. How ought I to praise Him that I
" escaped from the severe ordeal to serve Him, in the minis-
" try, for nearly half a century afterwards. My preaching
" was positive, unpliable, and authoritative; there was too
" much of severity and terror in it — too little consideration
"of my youth and inexperience, too little unction and gen-
"tleness."

From Locust street the Fifth Church moved to Arch street
above Tenth, and in that new field Dr. Skinner did the
noblest work of his life. Crowds flocked to hear him preach,
and when he announced a series of doctrinal sermons, had
the house been three times as large, it could not have held the
people who crowded to hear them. He continued there for
six months. The effect was profound and wide-spread. Tes-
timonies of confidence and sympathy were poured in from
men like Dr. Griffin, Dr. Richards, and Dr. Spring. Princeton smiled upon him, and by nomination of Dr. Green, in
the General Assembly, he was made a Director of that Seminary. For eight years longer he continued his ministry in
Arch street, when he accepted a call to the Pine street

Church, in Boston. From thence he went to Andover, and subsequently became pastor of the Mercer street Presbyterian Church, in New York. This charge he resigned in 1848 for a professor's chair in the Union Theological Seminary, in New York. He was now fifty-seven, and in this service he remained until he was eighty, when the Master called him to go up higher, and receive his reward.

JOSEPH SANFORD was the eighth pastor. Born in 1797, in Fairfield, Conn. At eight years of age he became a Christian, and made a public profession at thirteen. He early commenced studies for the ministry, and developed an uncommon talent for popular addresses. His labors in times of special religious interest were very acceptable, and greatly useful. He pursued his primary studies in Saratoga County, N. Y., and entered Union College in September, 1817. He studied theology at Princeton. In April, 1823, he was licensed by the Presbytery of New York, and went at once to Montreal, where he preached for some months to the American Presbyterian Church. In his short visit to that City, he endeared himself to God's people, and his labors were so acceptable that the church gave him a call, but he did not see his way clear to accept it. A call from Brooklyn, N. Y., soon followed, which he did accept, and was soon installed. Brooklyn was then rapidly growing, and soon became an important city. From the First Presbyterian Church, in Brooklyn, he was called, in September, 1828, to the Second Presbyterian Church, in Philadelphia. Dr. Janeway had resigned. The church embraced a large number of distinguished men, and had been blessed with a succession of able pastors. The prominence of the position, and the consequent responsibility of the post, induced the most careful thought and great hesitation. Drs. Green, Miller, Alexander, and McAuley, were sought as counsellors, and under advice of these fathers in the church, he at length decided on removal. He was installed January 21, 1829, and died December 25, 1831.

Like the men who had gone before, and into whose labors he entered, Mr. Sanford was eminent for piety. His conversation, his pulpit ministrations, his labors for his fellow men, marked him as a man of rare purity of character and much converse with God. Holiness was the fruit of his lips. He was much in prayer, and held daily converse with eternal things. In the pulpit, his prayers were marked with wonderful solemnity and unction. He seemed to be climbing the ladder for blessings for himself and his people. He grew in grace. It was not necessary to go to his intimate friends to learn his character — all who saw him and heard him, *felt* that he had been much with Jesus. He was *commanding as a speaker*, a voice of uncommon richness and compass. An agreeable countenance, great self-possession, and a master of the art of speaking, he was heard with profound attention. His addresses before the annual meetings of the great religious societies made deep and lasting impression. The ministry was his chosen and much loved work. In this he found his highest joy and greatest usefulness. He was consecrated to the work, and nothing could draw him aside from it. During his pastorate of this Church of less than three years, more than one hundred and fifty were added to the membership, and more than five hundred souls were brought to the knowledge of Christ in the two churches of which he was pastor. He followed in the line of mighty men — mighty men followed him.

For two years after his death the Church remained vacant. On the twenty-fifth of November, 1833, Rev. Cornelius C. Cuyler was called as the ninth pastor. Dr. Cuyler was a descendant of the colonists that settled the Province of New York as early as the time of Charles II. He was born at Albany, New York, in 1783, and trained under a mother who was left a widow when he was but twelve years of age. His mother was a woman of superior intellect and education, and eminent for her piety.

At fourteen young Cuyler was prepared for college. He graduated at Union in 1806, and at eighteen made a public profession of religion. His first purpose was to study law, but the change wrought in his heart and life by the Divine Spirit turned him at once to the ministry. He was licensed in 1808, and ordained and installed pastor of the Reformed Dutch Church in Poughkeepsie in 1809. From that Church he was called to Philadelphia in 1833, by unanimous vote of the Second Presbyterian Church. Frequent revivals marked his ministry in Poughkeepsie during the twenty-five years of his pastorate, and large additions were made to the Church. He was blessed of God, as the healer of strife as well as the winner of souls.

He entered upon his duties with this Church in the maturity of his strength and experience, and carried forward his work with the same earnest spirit and unshaken fidelity. The new field was unlike the old, from which so many spiritual harvests had been gathered. New difficulties, incident to life and change in a great city, gathered about his way. The Church was badly located, the drift of peoples and families was away from it, and farther to the west; and yet he wrought on with untiring zeal and ceaseless industry, in the pulpit, the Sabbath School, the prayer-meeting, the family circle, and found in all evident tokens of the Divine approval and blessing.   Gradual accessions were made to the Church, Christians were built up in the most holy faith, and the influence of the old historic church was felt for good on the neighboring Churches and throughout the City and the land.

He labored on for seventeen years, reaching the forty-third year of his ministry and the sixtieth of his life, when he resigned his pastorate.   At this time the disease which terminated his life had developed itself, and from that time till his death, August thirty-first, 1860, he had a constant struggle with suffering.   But in all his faith triumphed.   After the most solemn and tender counsels to his family, each member of which was addressed, and all committed to God in prayer, followed by some hours of uneasiness and fitful sleep, he was heard whispering the words : —

> " Where the Assembly ne'er breaks up,
> " The Sabbath ne'er shall end."—

and was gone.

Dr. Plumer, a friend, companion and fellow laborer in the Kingdom of God, says : —

"As a public servant of the Lord Jesus, he was entitled to great veneration. "He ever held fast the form of sound words. At no period of his ministry was "he suspected by good men of any defection from the truth. He was beyond all "charges of heterodoxy. But he did not rest in heartless orthodoxy. He ever "held that it was good to be zealously affected always in a good thing.

"He was among the most active and influential of all the friends of our "national benevolent societies. As he could he aided them during life.

"In the Presbyterian Church he was very greatly distinguished for the amount "of confidence and influence which he acquired while connected with it. He "has several times been a member of our highest Judicatory, and when there, "how wise and faithful he has been, the records will show and many will testify."

Dr. Gregory writes of a friend, now dead, who in writing of Dr. Cuyler's death, said : —

"The only perfect man I ever knew is gone — Dr. Cuyler "is dead."

His influence upon young men, and his zeal for their good, are exemplified in an instance which I will relate : —

"In the year 1847, a number of Presbyterians in Phœnixville, applied to the "Presbytery of Philadelphia, for an organization; but divisions arose among "them in reference to the doctrines of the Old and New School, and at a meet- "ing of Presbytery it was thought not worth while to look after them. Dr. Cuy- "ler, however, thought differently. He said there were precious souls there,

" and he would go and organize them.   During the services, he missed a young
"man whom he had seen at his first visit to the place.   He determined to see the
" young man.   He made inquiries at the house where the young man boarded,
" and was informed that he was at work in Montgomery County.   It was a
" bleak, cold morning, in the month of February, the snow and slush covered the
" ground to the depth of a foot or more ; but Dr. Cuyler, in spite of all obstacles,
" adhered to his determination to see this young man.   He started on his errand,
" and after a toilsome walk, discovered the object of his search.   He had a long
" talk with the young man, remonstrating with him for his evil ways, and begging
" him to return to the paths of duty.   The words of the good Doctor sank deep
" into the heart of the young man.   In less than one year he was ordained a
" Ruling Elder, and was the instrument, in the hands of God, in the course of
" six years, of organizing four Churches, all of which are to-day, prospering.   In
" several of these Churches he acted as Ruling Elder."

Dr. Cuyler resigned his charge in 1850.   The same year,
the Rev. CHARLES W. SHIELDS, was called as the tenth pastor.
He remained with the Church until 1865, when he resigned
his charge and accepted a professorship in Princeton College.
Dr. Shields still occupies that honorable and useful post.

Of his work in this Church it is not now the time to speak.
Greatly endeared to the people, he left many hearts, that could
not for a long time be reconciled to his departure, and who,
to this day, are steadfast in the loyalty of love.   As I knew
Dr. Shields in his boyhood, and have a profound admiration
for his superior talents, and his power as a preacher, I may

say this much — that he was eloquent and grand.   The most cultivated intellect, and the most ardent piety, could follow his rounded periods and majestic diction with delight.   With a native modesty, that amounted almost to diffidence, he shrank from the contact with men, and found it difficult to be at home, and at ease, in the work of pastoral visitation.   He was honored of God as a preacher of righteousness, and has left his name and his work as an inheritance among his brethren who wrought before him.   He kept the royal succession.

The eleventh pastor of the Second Church was installed, November 12, 1865, and is still on duty.

What will you do with this ancient heritage of God?

You have entered into other men's labors.   You are a ground that has been wet with the tears of Godly men and women, and upon which, the beaded sweat has fallen from the faces of men mighty in conflict and great in toil.   You sit under the vine and eat the fruit of trees which other hands have planted.   You hold the sacred trusts of the generations.

What will you do with them ? The future will hold you to strict account; and God, greater than all, will require at your hands the inheritance of your Father's unimpaired. You cannot squander this splendid patrimony, and be guiltless. You cannot allow this spotless record to be stained and bleared, and go blameless to the bar of God. The reaper's sickle will follow in your track, to gather either briars and thorns for the burning, or souls for the kingdom of God, as you shall sow the seed. What shall the harvest be ? What shall be the future of this Church, which God has honored for an hundred and thirty years, and made one of the gateways to His own Eternal Dwelling-place ? Give answer, ye men and women of Philadelphia, in noble deeds and saintly lives, and God shall crown your days and bless your work, as He has the hosts who have gone before you.

The Church Building,

[See Frontispiece.]

THE style of architecture is an adaptation of the thirteenth century — French Gothic, with some early English features. The plan consists of a lofty clere-story nave, with aisles and transepts, and a tower and spire at the north end of the west aisle. The nave terminates in an apse of five sides. The principal dimensions of the building are as follows, *viz :* — Length of nave, including apse, one hundred and nineteen feet; breadth across transepts, sixty-four feet, eight inches; breadth across nave and aisles, fifty-eight feet; height of nave from floor to crown of arched ceiling, sixty feet; height of ridge of nave roof (on exterior) above sidewalk, eighty feet; height of tower above sidewalk, one hundred and nine feet six inches; height of tower and spire, when finished, from sidewalk to top of stone finial, two hundred and two feet, and to the top of the iron corona, two hundred and nineteen feet.

The materials used on the exterior are Richmond granite for the base or plinth ; Trenton stone for the greater part of the walling above the plinth line ; Cleveland (Ohio) stone for the tracery of the windows, mouldings of the doorways, etc., together with red sandstone (Seneca quarries) from near Washington, D. C.; blue sandstone from Franklin, Venango county, Pa., and green serpentine from the Kilmarnock quarries, Delaware County, Pa., in special parts, for contrasts of color and decorative effects.

The interior of the building is faced, and the arches are built with buff-colored bricks, imported from England, similar to those made at Milwaukee.

In the windows throughout the building, the mullions are one-third the breadth of the lights next to them, and the tracery is in all cases placed in the centre of the thickness of the walls, so that strong shadows are produced. Much elaboration has been gone into on the two principal doorways. The west door is eleven feet in width of opening, and the top of finial of the gabled canopy over it, has an elevation of

thirty-six feet above the sidewalk. The mouldings of the
arch are rolls and hollows in clusters, separated by tooth
ornaments, which latter are continued down to the bases of
the columns. The capitals of the columns, supporting the
canopy, are covered with the rose, leek, thistle, and shamrock,
while the central column, dividing the door, has the four
united. The carving of the capitals, supporting the arch, represent flowers and ferns.

The tympanum of the door is of stone, boldly carved. In
the centre, within a vesica, is the text; "I am the Door," and
the sacred monograms, Chi, Rho and Alpha, Omega, and in the
spandrels around the vesica, the vine conventionally treated.

The tower door, although smaller, is treated in a manner
similar to the west door. The tympanum records the date of
the foundation of the Church, 1743.

The capitals of the columns represent the six leading agri-
cultural products of the country—wheat, corn, grapes, cotton,
tobacco and sugar,

The clere-story is lighted by lancets arranged in triplets,
and separated on the exterior by clustered columns of stone.

The mouldings throughout the interior are of terra-cotta and
of stone. No plaster is used in any part of the building.
The arches, supporting the clere-story, and dividing the nave

from the aisles and transepts, rest on polished shafts of native marbles, six different varieties being used. The capitals and bases of these columns are of light-colored free-stone, the plinths of black marble, and the dividing moulds or bands of white marble. Polished shafts are also used in pairs, forming corbels as responds to arches, and all the capitals are carved.

The nave roof is a barrel vault with arched wooden ceiling on moulded ribs, springing from the beams, and the arched ceiling continues at the same height around the apse. All the woodwork of the roof and ceiling is of yellow pine from Florida. The pulpit is of elaborate workmanship, and has been presented to the Church by Mr. Theodore Cuyler, in memory of the late Rev. Dr. Cuyler, for many years a pastor of this congregation. It is of Caen stone, and was executed by Messrs William Struthers & Sons. An angel, modeled by Mr. Bailey, the sculptor, forms the support of the pulpit, and the rest of the carving is by Mr. Calder. A baptismal font, (presented as a memorial to the late Mr. John Struthers, by Mr. William Struthers) and a communion table of black walnut, are placed on either side of the pulpit platform, and raised one step above the floor of the building. Black walnut has been used in the seating throughout the building, and crimson reps in the upholstery of the seats.

I

The gaslights are arranged in coronæ suspended in the arches. These have been made from designs of the architect. The organ was built by Messrs. W. B. D. Simmons & Co., of Boston, and cost $13,000. It is placed in a gallery at the Walnut street end of the nave, and is in two parts, the large west window, of four lights, being unobstructed. It has forty-four speaking stops, eight mechanical registers, six combination pedals, and two thousand nine hundred pipes.

APPENDIX.

ARCH STREET,

WITH SECOND PRESBYTERIAN CHURCH.

[See Plate opposite.]

THE extreme portion of the foreground is upon Arch street, near Fifth. On the south side a portion of the wall of Christ Church Burying Ground is seen. Adjoining and extending toward Fourth street, is a row of houses, some of which yet exist, and have been altered, the first stories being occupied as stores. This was one of the finest row of houses in the City, in the year 1800, and it was built by Wm. Sansom, a famous improver, who did much for the benefit of our local architecture; Mr. Sansom himself lived at this time in the house nearest the burying ground. His next door neighbor was Dr. Samuel Magaw, rector of St. Paul's Episcopal Church, and a Professor in the University of Pennsylvania; Andrew Hodge, Merchant; Thos. Steward-

son, Merchant, and Edward Thomson, occupied the houses
succeeding. The latter was subsequently the most famous
shipping merchant in the City, next to Stephen Girard. The
house at the south-west corner of Fourth and Arch streets,
was the residence in 1800, of Thos. W. Armat, Merchant.
It was built by the University of Pennsylvania, and occupied
for a time as the residence of the Provost. Rev. Wm. Smith
lived there in 1791, and in 1795 it was the residence of Rev.
John Ewing, Provost. At the north-west corner of Fourth
and Arch streets, the little two story building was a well accustomed tavern. John Whiteman kept it as the Sorrel Horse
in 1795, and J. Knight who succeeded him, put up the "Fox
and the Grapes," in 1800. Coming westward, from the corner, the houses on the north side of this street were occupied
successively by Ezra Varden, Tailor; John Flanagan, Printer,
and Samuel Parker, Brass Founder. The large house nearest
us was, in 1800, occupied by Dr. John Ewing, who had
moved from the south-west corner. At the north-east corner
of Fourth street, the fine, large, old fashioned house, which
still remains unaltered in the upper portion, was the residence
of the Keppele family until 1794. Jemima Carson kept it as
a boarding house in 1795, and Thos. Burke, Merchant, re-
sided there in 1800. Proceeding eastward on the north side,

we pass respectively the dwelling houses of Robert Rainey, Merchant; Leonard Kessler, Gentleman; Adam Walter, Shoe-maker; James Houston, Teller of the Bank of Pennsylvania; Gen. James Irwin, and the widow Loxley, at the corner of the court bearing her family name. At the other corner of the alley, was David Evans' carpenter shop; next was Valeria Fullerton's boarding house, the front room of which on the first floor was occupied by Wm. Sergeant, an eminent lawyer, and brother of the late Hon. John Sergeant, for his office. Jane Malcom's boarding house was next door to the residence of Alex. Wilcocks, who was then Recorder of the City of Philadelphia.

The Second Presbyterian Church was at the north-west corner of Arch and Third streets. It was a brick building, with windows with round heads, on Arch street. The foundation of this Meeting House was laid on the seventeenth of May, 1750, and the building was finished and dedicated on the thirty-first of May, 1752. The steeple was built by means of funds raised by a lottery, and was not finished until the latter part of 1763, or the beginning of 1764. It was a fine, large and showy construction, and a marked feature of observation from the approaches to the City. It became decayed after 1800, and the wooden portion was taken down,

and in 1809, the tower was torn down, and the space which
it occupied thrown into the body of the church. The last
sermon was preached in this church by Rev. Dr. Cuyler,
December 25, 1836, and the building was torn down shortly
afterward.

The street shows evidence of quietness; a few pedestrians
are seen. The gentleman with cane and fair top boots, on
the south side, keeps his fingers warm by hiding one hand
in his coat pocket. The two ladies are distinguished by their
fashionable bonnets. The servant at the pump, the negro
boy who watches the horses tied to the lamp post, the baker
with his cart, and the mechanic in trowsers and jacket, going
down Arch street, move leisurely, as if it were not proper to
be in a hurry. Even the hack and covered wagon coming
up, and the dray going down, seem to be driven in a delib-
erate manner as if there was plenty of time.

PASTORS.

GEORGE WHITEFIELD, ... FOUNDER.

GILBERT TENNENT, ... 1743

JOHN MURRAY, ... 1765

JAMES SPROAT, ... 1769

ASHBEL GREEN, ... 1787

J. N. ABEEL, ... 1794

JACOB J. JANEWAY, ... 1799

THOMAS H. SKINNER, ... 1813

JOSEPH SANFORD, ... 1828

CORNELIUS C. CUYLER, ... 1834

CHARLES W. SHIELDS, ... 1850

E. R. BEADLE, ... 1865

RULING ELDERS.

1745. — JAN.   16, .   CAPTAIN THOMAS BOURNE.
  "   "   "   SAMUEL HAZARD.

1746. — SEP.   25, .   .   GEORGE SPAFFORD.
  "   "   "   . . .   DAVID CHAMBERS.

1765. — FEB.   7, .   .   . JOHN WILLIAMS.
  "   "   "   . . . GUNNING BEDFORD.
  "   NOV.   14, ... JOHN RHEA.
  "   "   "   . .   . HUGH McCULLOUGH.
  "   "   "   . .   . ROBERT CATHER.
  "   "   "   . .   . DANIEL ROBERDEAU.
  "   "   "   . .   .   . JOHN McCALLA.

1784. —   .   .   . DR. JOHN REDMAN.
  "   .   .   . EBENEZER HAZARD.
  "   .   .   . COL. JOHN BAYARD.

1789. — MARCH 7, .   . WILLIAM FALCONER.
  "   "   "   .   . ISAAC SNOWDEN.

1790. — MAY   15,   WILLIAM BROWN.
  "   "   "   .   . ROBERT SMITH.
  "   JUNE   5, .   .   . SAMPSON HARVEY.

1802. — DEC.   4,   .   .   .   ROBERT RALSTON.
  "   "   "   .   .   .   JOHN HARRIS.
  "   "   "   .   THOMAS LATIMER.
  "   "   "   .   .   .   . DANIEL JAUDON.

1818. — JAN.   20,   .   .   . ALEXANDER HENRY.
  "   "   "   .   .   .   . ISAAC SNOWDEN.

1827. — APRIL 9, ...   JOHN MOORE.
  "   "   "   .   .   .   ANDREW BROWN.
  "   "   "   .   . ROBERT HOBART SMITH.
  "   "   "   .   . MATTHEW L. BEVAN.

1837. — APRIL 17,   GEORGE H. VAN GELDER.
  "   "   "   .   .   .   CHARLES COLLINS.

1841. — JAN.   19,   .   . DR. WILLIAM DARRACH. ʋ
  "   "   "   .   . BENJAMIN STILLÉ.
  "   "   "   .   .   .   WILLIAM NASSAU.
  "   "   "   .   .   .   . WILLIAM DULLY.

1852. — NOV.   24, ... JOEL JONES.
  "   "   "   .   . WILLIAM R. THOMPSON.
  "   "   "   .   . CHARLES MACALESTER.
  "   "   "   .   .   CHARLES E. MORGAN.

| 1862.—Jan. | 5, | . | . | Dr. WILLIAM DARRACH. |
| " | " | " | . | . THOMAS M. FREELAND. |

1869.—Nov.	8,	.	.	H. LENOX HODGE, M. D.
"	"	"	. . . .	. M. S. STOKES.
"	"	"	. . . .	. H. W. PITKIN.
"	"	"	.	. CHARLES F. HASELTINE.

| 1876.—Jan. | 2, | . | . | JOHN G. READING. |
| " | " | " | . : . . | . PAUL GRAFF. |

DEACONS, 1877.

A. B. WALTERS.
WILLIAM T. CARTER.
GEORGE HUNT.
DAVID LEE.
JAMES M. EARLE.
WILLIAM L. MACTIER.
JOHN P. LOGAN.

TRUSTEES, 1876.

EXTRACTS FROM CHARTERS.

" *Thomas Penn and John Penn, true and absolute proprietaries of the*
" *Province of Pennsylvania and Counties of New Castle, Kent, and Sussex,*
" *on Delaware, to all persons to whom these presents may come,* GREETING : —

    *   *   *   *   *   *   *

" Wherefore, they have prayed us to incorporate the committee of said Church,
" by the name of the Trustees of the Second Presbyterian Church, in the City
" of Philadelphia, in the Province of Pennsylvania ; and that they and their
" successors, by such name, may be erected and constituted a body politic and
" corporate, and have perpetual succession.   Now know ye, that we, favoring
" the prayer and application of the said elders, deacons, and members, and
" willing as much as in us lies to encourage, virtue, piety, and charity, and for
" other good causes and considerations, us thereto specially moving, have nom-
" inated, ordained, and appointed Samuel Smith, Andrew Hodge, John Redman,
" Hugh McCulloch, William Shippen, sr., William Henry, William Shippen, jr.,
" Nathan Cooke, Gunning Bedford, John Bayard, Jedediah Snowden, Joseph
" Reed, William Hollingshead, William Carson, John Hall, William Bradford,
" Robert Harris, John Rhea, Isaac Snowden, Jonathan B. Smith, Benjamin
" Armitage, William Drury, Benjamin Harbison, and David Chambers, to be
" the first Trustees of the Second Presbyterian Church in the City of Phila-
" delphia."

    *   *   *   *   *   *   *
    *   *   *   *   *   *   *

" *Witness* RICHARD PENN, ESQ., Lieutenant Governor and Commander-in
" Chief of our said Province, at Philadelphia, the day and year aforesaid."

    [L. S.]   " RICHARD PENN.

" Enrolled in the Rolls Office in and for the Province of Pennsylvania, in
" Patent Book A A, vol. 12, page 99, &c."

" Witness my hand and seal of office, the 18th day of November, 1772."

                                        " WILLIAM PARR,

         [L. S.]   "*Rec.*"

There is also, afterwards, an Act, entitled, "An Act for re-establishing the
" Charter of the Second Presbyterian Church, in the City of Philadelphia, and
" for other purposes therein mentioned." It reads thus : —

" *Whereas:*—The Second Presbyterian Congregation, in the City of Philadelphia,
" by their petition, have shown, that by their Charter of Incorporation, bearing
" date the twenty-fourth day of August, in the year of our Lord, one thousand
" seven hundred and seventy-two, granted by the Honorable Richard Penn, esq.,
" then being Lieutenant-Governor of Pennsylvania, twenty-four persons therein
" named, members of the said congregation, and their successors, were nom-
" inated and ordained, and appointed to be the trustees of the Second Presby-
" terian Church, in the City of Philadelphia, etc."

" SEC. 2. — And whereas the said congregation have further shown, that by
" reason of many of their members having withdrawn themselves from their
" places of residence in the City on the prospect of the enemy's approach, and
" by reason of the enemy having since been in actual possession of the City and
" of their Church, the said annual elections were prevented from being held,
" so that no more than eight trustees remain, by which means there cannot be a
" quorum capable of doing any business ; and have further shown, that by
" experience they find that their having so large a quorum as thirteen renders

" it at all times very difficult to procure a board for doing business. And also,
" that in and by the said Charter, it is provided that the clear yearly value of
" the real estate of the said corporation shall not exceed the sum of three
" hundred pounds, sterling money of Great Britain, for each house of public
" worship erected, or to be erected, by the said corporation, which sum is
" inadequate to the pious and humane purposes intended, and have therefore
" prayed, etc."

" SEC. 3.—*Be it therefore enacted, and it is hereby enacted, by the Representa-*
" *tives of the Freemen of the Commonwealth of Pennsylvania in General As-*
" *sembly met, and by the authority of the same, etc., etc.* * * And that Joseph
" Reed, Thomas Bourne, Andrew Hodge, Gunning Bedford, John Bayard,
" Hugh Hodge, William Faulkner, William Smith, Isaac Snowden, Daniel
" Goodman, Benjamin Harbison, Nathan Cook, William Geddis, Jared Inger-
" soll, William Hollingshead, James Hunter, Samuel McClane, James Robeson,
" Abraham Dubois, Hugh Lenox, Jonathan B. Smith, Thomas Nevill, William
" McIlhenny, and Joseph Eastburne, last elected to be Trustees, as aforesaid,
" be, and they are hereby declared to be, the present Trustees of the said
" Church."   *   *   *   *   *   *

> (Signed)   "JOHN BAYARD,
> "*Speaker.*"

" Enacted into a law at Philadelphia, on Friday, the third of March, A. D.
" 1780."

> "THOMAS PAINE,
> "*Clerk of the General Assembly.*"

OFFSHOOTS FROM THE
Second Presbyterian Church of Philadelphia.

The following abstracts have been made from Histories compiled by Mr. Samuel Agnew, *of the Presbyterian Historical Society, from the original books and papers:—*

FIRST CHURCH OF THE NORTHERN LIBERTIES.

ABOUT 1764, the Rev. Dr. Sproat commenced stated preaching at Campington, in a small frame house provided for the purpose by the Second Church. The building was known by the name of "The Old Cannon House," and was at the North-east corner of Coates and St. John streets. Eventually Drs. Green and Janeway, aided by Robert Ralston, solicited funds sufficient to erect a brick building, eighty by sixty feet, at the North-west corner of Coates and Second streets, which was first opened for worship,

on Sabbath, April 7, 1805, the pulpit was supplied by the
Pastor of the Second Church down to April 20, 1813, when
it was separated from the Second Church by the Presbytery
of Philadelphia, and constituted a distinct congregation, under
the name of "The Church of the Northern Liberties."

The formal organization of the Church was January 12,
1814.   The first Pastor was the Rev. James Patterson.   "The
"property becoming valuable and inconveniently noisy, it was
"thought advisable to pull down this building, and the congre-
"gation removed to another location."   (*Communication of
"Mr. Samuel Hazard, to the Board of Trustees of Second
"Church.*")

This Church is now in Buttonwood street, below Sixth
street.

THE TABERNACLE; OR,
SEVENTH PRESBYTERIAN CHURCH.

At a meeting of the Session of the Second Presbyterian
Church, held October 4, 1804, a letter was presented from
nine members of the Church, requesting dismissal.   These
members were originally of the "Independent persuasion,"
and desired now, with others, entertaining similar sentiments,

to form an Independent Church. The nine members were:—
William Shufflebottom, William Sheepshanks, Charles Wood-
ward, Robert Murphey, John Lorain, jr., Gilbert Gaw,
Susannah Gaw, John Firth, and Elizabeth Firth.

"In a short time they were so much prospered, that they
"purchased a lot and built a House of Worship, which as to
"situation, neatness and convenience, is not surpassed by any
"in Philadelphia. To this an additional lot was procured in
"Cherry street, near the south-east corner of Fifth street, from
"Schuylkill, of one hundred and thirty-two feet front on Cherry
"street, and one hundred and forty-four feet in depth, which is
"appropriated to the use of the congregation as a place of
"interment." (*Minute Book of the Second Reformed Dutch
Church in the City of Philadelphia, December, 1816.*)

Eleven years later the congregation having been long without a Pastor, and having met with many difficulties, a Congregational Meeting was called, and it was resolved that overtures
should be made to the people of the First Reformed Dutch
Church, in Crown street, to unite with the body to which they
belonged. On July 1, 1816, this Independent Congregation,
together with some persons from the First Dutch Church,
formed the Second Reformed Dutch Church.

. At a meeting of the Presbytery of Philadelphia, held in

J

Abington, November 9, 1819, an application from the congregation lately styled the Second Reformed Dutch Church in the City of Philadelphia, was made through William Sheepshanks, Robert Hamill and Thomas Whitacar, Commissioners appointed for said purpose to the Presbytery of Philadelphia, that said congregation be taken under the care of the Presbytery with a view to be duly organized as the Seventh Presbyterian Church in the City of Philadelphia. (*Minutes of Presbytery of Philadelphia.*)

November 18, 1819.—The Seventh Presbyterian Church was organized by Rev. Drs. Neill, Ely and Janeway, with Messrs. Robert Ralston and John McMullin, a committee appointed for the purpose by the Presbytery.

This Church now worships in the building on Broad street, above Chestnut.

—

FIFTH PRESBYTERIAN; OR, ARCH STREET CHURCH.

At a meeting of the Presbytery of Philadelphia, held March 3, 1813, in the Second Presbyterian Church, a petition was received from George Durfer and others, requesting to be erected into a Fifth Presbyterian Church. The subject was referred to a committee, who at the stated meeting of Presbytery, April 21, 1813, reported at length, giving the leading facts, setting forth this and other particulars:—"That the "petition proceeded from a large number of individuals who "had belonged to the Evangelical Congregation of the City "and vicinity of Philadelphia, etc., etc., etc."

The Presbytery granted their petition, and appointed Rev. Mr. Potts to organize them into a regular Presbyterian Church.

"On the last Lord's Day, the new meeting house of the "Fifth Presbyterian Congregation (in Locust street,) was "opened for public worship." (*Religious Remembrancer*, *June 3, 1815.*)

November 27, 1816.—At a meeting of Presbytery, held this day, a call from the Fifth Presbyterian Church was put into the hands of the Rev. Thomas H. Skinner, the Associate Pastor of the Second Presbyterian Church. The call was accepted and he was installed, December 1, 1816.

"*Sessional Records of the Second Presbyterian Church of Philadelphia, December 13, 1816.*"

"A letter received from several members of the congrega-
"tion, in full communion with the Church, dated thirteenth
"ult., requesting a dismission from the communion of the
"Church, was read. Whereupon it was resolved, that their
"request be granted, and that the following certificate be given
"them, *viz.:*—

"By virtue of an agreement entered into, on fifth Novem-
"ber, 1816, between the friends of the Rev. T. H. Skinner,
"and the congregation of the Second Presbyterian Church,
"those who were desirous of withdrawing, should have an
"honorable dismissal, and a written request being made to
"the session by the persons hereafter named to that effect,
"they are hereby dismissed as being in good standing with
"the Second Presbyterian Church, to join such Church or
"Churches as God in his providence may direct."

Isaac Ashmead,	John H. Scudder,	Alexander Anderson,
Mary R. Mitchell,	Charles Thompson,	Jane Phillips,
Pierce Chamberlain,	Jared Bunce,	Mary Ann Hodgdon,
Eliza Darrach,	Caroline Hutchins,	Ann Jane Ramsey,
Charlotte Darrach,	Mary Vance,	Susan B. Bradford,

Ann Parkhill,

Francis F. Fairbairn,

Hannah Clark,

Elizabeth Harbeson,

Augusta Anderson,

Thomas Bradford, jr.,

Eliza Bradford,

William Bradford,

Daniel Thatcher,

John Hansom,

Samuel Lloyd,

Mary Ann Bunce,

Hannah Bason,

Hannah Brown,

Ann Johnson,

Catharine Graham,

Judith Smith,

Elizabeth Work,

Sarah Evans,

Catharine Smith,

Constance Frinck,

Charles McCalla,

Elizabeth Smith,

Susan Boyle,

Ann Ruth,

Madelaine Barnes,

Jane Graham,

Thomas Snowden,

Thomas D. Mitchell,

Elizabeth Ruth,

Julianna Ruth,

Elizabeth Bulkley,

Mary Cook.

February 1, 1817, by a letter dated November 28, 1816:—

Mary Pearson,

Nichodemus Lloyd,

Ann Vanderwarter,

Elizabeth Clark.

January 29, 1817.—The minutes of the Session of the Fifth Presbyterian Church record the admission of the foregoing fifty-two communicants, giving their names in detail.

This exodus from the Second Church, with the Associate Pastor, Dr. Skinner, almost made the Fifth Church a new congregation.

Afterwards the people built, for Dr. Skinner, a handsome Church, which still exists in Arch street, above Tenth.

NORTH PRESBYTERIAN CHURCH.

From the Minutes of the Presbytery of Philadelphia:—

"April 20, 1825.—A petition from one hundred and four
"subscribers, principally residing in the Northern Liberties,
"was presented, requesting that they might be taken under
"the care of Presbytery, and organized as a Presbyterian
"Church; which request was granted, and Dr. Green, Mr.
"Patterson, and Mr. Alexander Henry were appointed a
"Committee, etc."

"October 19, 1825. — The Committee reported that they
"had organized the Church, 'to be known as the Second
"'Presbyterian Church in the Northern Liberties.'"

"A call for Rev. James Smith, from the Second Presby-
"terian Church in the Northern Liberties, was presented,
"which, being found in order, was put into his hands, and
"he signified his acceptance of the same."

The Rev. James Smith, prior to his official work in this
organization, worshipped with the Second Church, in Arch
street. He states that the Church now known as the North
Church, on Sixth street, above Green, owes its existence
more directly to the efforts of the late Robert Ralston (an

elder of the Second Church, in Arch street) than to any one else.

"He first proposed to me to make the attempt of erecting "that building. It was at the close of a social prayer meeting, "which had been held on that occasion in the house of the "late Alexander Henry (also an elder of the Second Church,) "when Mr. Ralston invited me to call at his office in the "following morning, and said that he would then give me "his name for a subscription to the erection of a new church "edifice in the northern part of the City."

Mr. Ralston made out for him a written statement of the object intended, gave him a subscription, and actively aided him in obtaining other subscriptions.

The building was commenced in the Spring of 1828.

On October 27, 1831, the minutes of Presbytery show that application was made by thirty-nine members of the First Presbyterian Church of Northern Liberties (which also came out of the Second Church, in Arch street, as shown above,) to be organized as the Third Presbyterian Church in Northern Liberties. This application, after examination, was granted, and Drs. Green, Skinner, and Rev. Mr. Grant were appointed a Committee to organize them. The Church worshipped in a school house, in Poplar street, near Second.

About the close of the year 1832, the Second and Third Presbyterian Churches in the Northern Liberties united under the name of the First Presbyterian Church in Penn Township, and the Rev. Hugh M. Koontz became the pastor. The united congregation occupied the building begun in 1828, by the Second Presbyterian Church in the Northern Liberties, and partially finished, on Sixth street, above Green. It is now known as the North Church.

ELEVENTH; OR, WEST ARCH STREET PRESBYTERIAN CHURCH.

The late Wilfred Hall, who died a communicating member of the Second Church, was one of the founders of the Eleventh Church, and stated that the parties originating and organizing this Church were all members of the congregation of the Second Church.

The Session Book of the West Arch Street Church states that "the first meeting on behalf of the enterprise was held in "the Lecture Room of the Second Presbyterian Church, "March 29th, 1828, and was called by Edward Sprague, Wil-

"liam Wallace, Charles McCalla, Robert Street, James Wilson,
"Joseph W. Martin, Wilfred Hall, Jacob Eldridge, and James
"Hunt, when it was resolved to organize a Presbyterian
"Church, and to take means for the erection of a suitable
"building in the north-western section of the City."

"*From the Sessional Records of the Second Church.*"

"November 21, 1828. — An application was read from the
"undersigned members of this Church, for a dismission, to
"unite with a Presbyterian Church, to be located, and now
"forming, in Vine street, near Thirteenth street, in this City."

Jacob Eldridge and wife,	James Wilson,
Wilfred Hall,	Hiram Ayres,
Elizabeth White,	John Umstead and wife,
William Wallace,	Joseph W. Martin.

"The request of which it was agreed to comply with, and
"the Clerk be directed to issue certificates accordingly."

, The records of the Presbytery of Philadelphia show that
October 21, 1828, a petition was presented for the organization
of a new Church, near the corner of Vine and Twelfth streets.
Dr. Green, Dr. Skinner, and Rev. J. C. Potts, were appointed
a Committee to act.

On August 13, 1829, a call was presented to Mr. John L. Grant, who signified his acceptance of the same. He was installed Pastor, November 18, 1829.

"The congregation first worshipped in the Franklin Insti-"tute, Seventh street, south of Market, and when they went "to Vine there was no other building on the whole square, "from Twelfth to Thirteenth streets."

The present edifice on the corner of Arch and Eighteenth streets was dedicated on Sunday, October 15, 1855.

CENTRAL PRESBYTERIAN CHURCH.

The Central Presbyterian Church originated in the withdrawal of a large number of members from the Second Church soon after the death of the Rev. Joseph Sanford, Pastor of the Church.

"The congregation was organized May 21, 1832, in the "Franklin Institute.   *   *   *   The Church was "organized on nineteenth day of June following, in the White-"field Academy, in Fourth street.   *   *   *   At "this meeting Messrs. Alexander Henry and Matthew L.

" Bevan, who had been Ruling Elders in the Second Church,
"were elected and installed Elders in the Central Church.
" Nineteen members, all on certificate from the Second Church,
"constituted the infant organization." (*Synopsis of History
of the Central Church, prepared for that Church, March 1,
1869.*)

" *Sessional Records of Second Church.*"

"June 15, 1832. — Session met at Dr. Green's study. The
"following application was submitted : — ' The undersigned
"' communicants of the Second Presbyterian Church, respect-
"' fully request of the Session that certificates of dismissal,
"' for the purpose of attaching themselves to such other
"' sister Church as in the Providence of God may be deemed
"' best.' Philadelphia, June 12, 1832."

Alexander Henry,	Sarah E. Davidson,	Debby Bevan,
Hannah M. Henry,	Mary E. Heberton,	Matthew L. Bevan,
Anna Maria Henry,	John V. Cowell,	F. V. King,
Letitia Henry Smith,	Hannah Cowell,	Martha C. King,
Ann M. Richards,	Mary Cowell,	Rufus L. Barnes,
Mary Davidson,	Jane Tate,	Ann Barnes.

The Session ordered the Clerk to make out certificates for
each.

In October, 1832, the Central Church received an accession of one hundred and twenty-seven members. All were on certificate from the Second Church, with the exception of five.

On June 22, 1832, at a meeting of the Session of the Second Church, applications were received from one hundred and twenty-five members of the Church for dismission. The Clerk was authorized to make out certificates for each applicant, to join " such other Church as the Providence of God may seem " to direct."

The following are the names : —

David T. Riesch,	M. Garnett,	Elizabeth Prentiss,
Nancy Reynolds,	George H. Van Gelder,	Mary Perkins,
Margaret Monell,	Henry Bill,	Sarah Durborr,
Elizabeth Gundelach,	Martha Gatter,	Theresa Shoemaker,
C. H. Gundelach,	John Vanarsdale,	Ann Shippen,
Michael Renwalls,	Peter L. Alrich,	Triphemia Otis,
Ellen A. Renwalls,	Sarah Walker,	Jane Williams,
Mary Beak,	Ambrose Walker,	Jane Hart,
Ann Beak,	John C. Moore,	Rebecca Branson,
Mary Sands,	Peter Lees,	Ann Robison,
Alleta Crawley,	Mary Lees,	Elizabeth Davis,
Martha Slack,	John Kennedy,	Sarah Loder,
Martha Strawback,	Theodosia Kennedy,	Elizabeth Culp,
Flora Scudder,	George Fithian,	Margaret Rhees,
Charlotte P. Brooke,	Mary Fithian,	Mary Johnson,

Sarah B. Richards,
Mary Garrosen,
Mrs. R. B. Aertson,
Mary S. Christie,
Sarah Sparks,
Tabitha Clark,
Mary Fowler,
Sarah Nash,
Eliza P. Barr,
Ann Bail,
Jane B. Wilson,
Margaret R. Barr,
Theodosia Bayard,
Jane M. Robinson,
Maria Tatem,
Martha Wellman,
Susannah Gaw,
Rebecca Gaw,
Elizabeth J. Henry,
Eliza J. Garnett,
Harriet Garnett,
Mary Ann Van Tine,
Ellen Schott,
Mary Ann Gordon,
Elizabeth King,
George Pierson,

E. R. Johnson,
Charity Johnson,
Priscilla Stewart,
Martha Pierson,
Elizabeth Hamilton,
Robert Sheppard,
Maria Sheppard,
Sarah Stinefeltz,
Arabella Watts,
Mary McDowell,
Lydia L. Miller,
Ann Allen,
Sarah C. Donnell,
Loetitia Howell,
Elizabeth H. Moore,
Isabella B. Davis,
Mary Farley,
Ann Jane Smith,
Eve Morris,
John McDaniel,
Abraham Crawley,
Ann Watts,
Rebecca McCalla,
Phœbe Clark,
Letitia Clark,
Sarah Clark,
Mary Henry,

Hannah Lawrence,
John H. Campbell,
Catharine Campbell,
Margaret Garnett,
Elizabeth White,
Ann M. Albertie,
Ann Hillis,
Frances Mitchell,
Margaret Milldrum,
Anna M. Woglom,
Mary Burkhart,
Eunice W. Thatcher,
Sarah Olmstead,
Sarah Harbeson,
Sarah P. Robinson,
Elizabeth Dexter,
Mary Foreman,
Ann Crosby,
Agnes Goodhary,
Harriet Perkins,
Elizabeth Bishing,
William Wallace,
Mary A. Carroll,
Hannah Roberts,
Elizabeth Snyder,
Ellen Wallace.

The congregation worshipped in the Whitefield Academy, in Fourth street, until the completion of their own house of worship, on the corner of Eighth and Cherry streets.

The Church was received under the care of the Presbytery, April 18, 1833, and Dr. John McDowell, of Elizabethtown, N. J., was installed the first Pastor, June 6, 1833.

THE CONGREGATIONAL SCHOOLS.

"The Church not occupying the whole space purchased "on Third street, in 1749, left a vacancy there, on a part of "which, and a lot adjoining, purchased by the congregation, "was erected John Ely's frame school house, to which most "of the boys of the Church were sent. This school house, "about the year 1794, gave place to a three-story brick build-"ing, erected by the congregation for a lecture room and "charity schools of the Church, which was afterwards sold "with the rest of the Church property." (*Communication to Trustees, by S. Hazard.*)

" Extracts from the Resolutions of the Board of Trustees respect-
" ing the organization of the Congregational School."

" Part of SEC. 2. — That a Committee be appointed to receive applications
" for the admission of Scholars, and to direct such admission when they deem
" it proper: And their order, in writing, to the Master, shall be his sufficient
" and sole warrant for receiving Scholars into the School."

" SEC. 4. — That all the members of the Congregation be entitled to send
" their children to the School; and that not only such as hold pews or seats
" in the Church, but all who worship statedly there, shall, for this purpose,
" be considered as members of the Congregation."

" That the children of such members of the Congregation as are unable to
" pay for their education be admitted in preference to any others, and taught
" free of any expence; and, if necessary, that they be also furnished with books
" gratis: And, that three dollars per quarter (or a less sum at the discretion
" of the Committee) shall be paid for the tuition of others who shall be ad-
" mitted into the School."

" SEC. 5. — Should any monies due for tuition be in arrear a fortnight after
" the quarter bills shall have been sent in, the Committee may thereupon
" exclude the children of the delinquents from the School, unless, on exam-
" ination of the case, they shall find satisfactory reasons for giving further
" indulgence, making an abatement, or relinquishing the claim of payment
" altogether."

" SEC. 8. — That the Minister, or Ministers, of our Congregation, shall, at
" all times, have free access to the School; and, with the approbation of the
" Committee, shall direct in what manner the religious instruction of the
" Scholars shall be conducted."

"SEC. 9.—That, as it is probable, that charitably disposed persons will
"make donations and bequests for the use of the School, the Committee have
"authority to receive such donations and bequests, and apply them as intended
"by the donors."

"Extract from the Minutes,

"ROBERT SMITH, Sec'ry."

"FORM OF A BEQUEST OF PERSONAL ESTATE FOR THE
"USE OF THE ABOVE INSTITUTION."

"*I give and bequeath to the* Trustees of the Second Presbyterian Church
"in Philadelphia, *for the Congregational School under the care of the said*
"*Trustees, the sum of*

"FORM OF A BEQUEST OF REAL ESTATE."

"*I give and bequeath to the* Trustees of the Second Presbyterian Church
"in the City of Philadelphia, *and to their successors forever, for the use of*
"*the Congregational School under the care of the said Trustees, etc.* (Here
"insert a description of the property bequeathed."

"CONGREGATIONAL SCHOOL:"

"THE Trustees finding that the present plan of the CONGREGATIONAL "SCHOOL, will not admit as many scholars as offer, which has occasioned "disappointments to many of the congregation who wished to have their "children instructed there, have determined to engage an assistant for the "present teacher; which, at the same time that it will enable them to receive "a greater number, will secure to each child a greater portion of the instructors' "attention than can be given under the existing regulations, additional scholars "can be immediately admitted; and although employing an usher will add "considerably to their expences, the Trustees charge but four dollars per quar- "ter for tuition; which will also be the price after the expiration of the present "quarter for the full pay scholars now in the school."

"April 20, 1803."

Philadelphia : — Printed by Jane Aitken, No. 20, North Third street.

From Report of a Special Committee of the Second Presby- terian Church of Philadelphia. Exhibiting a general view of its financial concerns. Report adopted April 12, 1832.

"With reference to the Congregational Schools, your committee have exam- "ined the minutes of 1826, and find, that in May of that year, the annual "appointment of the School Committee was suspended, and a Special Com-

K

" mittee of investigation appointed, consisting of Messrs. Jaudon, Moore,
" Bevan, Brown, and Lesley, to examine and report the state of the School.
" In their report, accepted and approved by the Board, June 12, they express
" their 'unanimous opinion that there should be an entire and radical change
" 'in our whole system respecting it.' In consequence of this, the Board
" suspended the operation of the School in its Congregational character. At
" this time, there were nineteen children in the School receiving gratuitous
" education, at the expence of the fund. These, with the pay scholars that
" remained, were immediately placed under the temporary care of the Rev.
" John L. Grant, who kindly offered his services gratuitously, until a compe-
" tent teacher could be obtained."

    " The Committee subsequently determined, that until a more favourable oppor-
" tunity presented for the re-organization of the Congregational School, they
" would confine their care, more immediately, to the instruction of our gratis
" children; for this purpose they entered into an agreement with Archibald
" Mitchell, a gentleman of standing as a teacher, to give instruction to our
" boys at the rate of $16 each, per ann. in addition to the usual charges for
" stationary, &c. and also with Mrs. Robinson, for the instruction of the girls,
" at the same rate. This plan for the appropriation of the funds, has been
" continued to the present time, with but little variation. In 1828 the Com-
" mittee found it necessary to adopt a resolution, which received the sanction
" of the Board, requiring that the applicant for the tuition of a child, or depen-
" dent, be at least three years a pewholder, next preceding the application,
" before he could receive the benefit of the fund. The present situation of
" the funds is exhibited in the report of the Committee, approved April 5, 1832.
" In this, the Committee state, that 'the balance on hand is $197 10, which
" 'the committee suggest be invested, as heretofore, in stock, for the benefit of

" 'the Congregational School.'   The investments made from the savings of th e
" fund since 1827, 'are —

" ' Twenty-six shares of North Amer. Insurance stock, at 92½ per ct., $240 50
" ' Pennsylvania 5 per cent. Loan, ...   122 80
" ' Which, with the above balance of . . . . . . · 197 10

" ' Makes a total of income saved of $560 40

" ' Though the number now on the list is comparatively small, yet the com-
" ' mittee believe, that the benefit of the fund has not been withheld from any
" ' applicant justly entitled thereto.'   'The sources from which the School in-
" ' come are derived are the following : —

" ' Sixty-six shares of North America Insurance stock, par value, . $ 660 00
" ' Pennsylvania State Fives, ... · . . .   122 80
" ' Amount loaned to the Church at six per cent.,. 1,677 77
" ' And the rents of the School House back of the Church.' "

" The committee making the above report are Messrs. Cole, White, Hodge,
" Macalester and Lesley."

" A re-organization of the Congregational School in the building back of the
" Church is eminently deserving an early attention of the Board; it might,
" and in all probability would become, as in times past, an auxiliary to the
" Church, as in it, strong attachments both to the Church and its officers would
" be formed, while by the use of the Scriptures as a reading book, and the
" catechisms of the Presbyterian church, our youth would be preserved from
" the errors which so much abound."

COPIES OF EPITAPHS

IN THE OLD BRICK BUILDING, ARCH AND THIRD STREETS.

———

"Hoc sub marmore conduntur Reliquiæ
GILBERTI TENNENT,
Hujus Ecclesiæ Pastoris primi,
Cujus maximè operâ
Ædes hæcce,
Deo sacra,
Ad summum perducta fuerit.
Patre Gulielmo Tennent oriundus
Armachæ Hibernorum natus,
Nonis Feb. MDCCII
Novæ Brunsviæ Pastor electus,
MDCCXXV,
Indidem Philadelphiam evocatus,
MDCCXLIII,
Obiit X. Kal. Feb. MDCCLXIV,
Annum agens LXII.

Vir fuit prudens, consultus venerabilis,
Moribus et Pietate spectabilis,
Conjux, Frater, Pater et Amicus,
Inter præstantissimos :
Veræ Religionis Propugnator
Acerrimus, doctus, fidelis, secundus.
      Et denique,
   Christianus sine fuco extitit.
   Hoc Elogio decorandum
   Curarunt Ecclesiæ Cœtus
   Sui quondam Auditores."

[By President Finley.]

"Here are deposited
The remains of
SAMUEL FINLEY, D. D.,
He was born in the County of Armagh, in Ireland,
A. D. 1715 :
Arrived at Philadelphia Sept. 28th, 1734 :
Was ordained a minister in 1743 :
Settled in 1744, at West Nottingham ;
Where in an academy which he established,
He qualified many youths for future usefulness.
He was removed in July, 1761,
To Princeton in New Jersey,
As President of the College there.

Was created Doctor in Divinity by the University
Of Glasgow, in 1763;
And died in Philadelphia, July 16th, 1766.
In life he was a pattern of excellence,
And, animated by the supporting consolations
Of the Gospel,
He exhibited, in death,
A bright Example of triumphant Faith."

[By Hon. Ebenezer Hazard.]

" Sacred to the memory of
THE REV. JAMES SPROAT, D. D.,
Who was born at
Scituate in the State of Massachusetts,
April 11th, 1721, O. S.
Educated at the College of Yale,
Ordained a minister of the Gospel
At Guilford, in the State of Connecticut,
August 23rd, 1743.
Translated to this Church
March 30th, 1769.
Died of the yellow fever
October 18th, 1793,
In the 73rd year of his age and 51 of his ministry.

Whatever is guileless,
Candid and benevolent,
In the human Character,
Was conspicuous in his.
Amiable in domestic life,
Fervent in Piety,
Mighty in the Scriptures,
Powerful in Prayer,
Plain, practical and evangelical
      In preaching,
Eminent in Tenderness and Charity for others,
Humble in his views of himself,
He was beloved and respectable as a man,
Useful and venerable as a minister of Christ."

[Written by Rev. Ashbel Green.]

"On a marble under the pulpit as are also the foregoing epitaphs of Tennent "and Finley, there are the remains and a stone, with an inscription, but in "a situation not easily to be read, of Rev. Josiah Smith, of Bermuda, Cainhoy, "and who died in Philadelphia."

THE BURIAL PLACES OF THE SECOND CHURCH.

— -

MIDDLE AISLE OF CHURCH AT THIRD AND ARCH STREETS.

The Rev. Gilbert Tennent was buried "with much decency "in the front aisle of his own Church." "In front of the "pulpit were his body, with those of the Rev. Dr. Finley "and of the Rev. Mr. Smith. These two, also buried there, "were removed to the burying ground in Arch street, above "Fifth, when the Church was altered in 1809, and deposited "under the west end. They were placed in one bin, the "bones being on removal so intermingled as to forbid sep- "aration. They were afterwards all removed by the grand- "daughter, Miss Elizabeth Smith, to Abingdon, to be interred "alongside her mother, his daughter. There was also re-

"moved to the burying ground a marble on Dr. Sproat, as
"he was interred at his death in the ground, in 1793, and *not*
"in the Church." *

The tombstones of these Pastors were laid in the middle
aisle of the Church.   Copies of the inscriptions upon the
stones are given in this book, (page 156.)

BURYING GROUNDS IN ARCH STREET AND IN NOBLE STREET.

Mr. Samuel Hazard, in a communication to the Board of
Trustees, upon his retirement from that Board, in 1864,
says : —

"The burying ground at Arch, above Fifth, was purchased
"in 1750, from Thomas Leach and others, fifty feet on Arch
"street, and three hundred and six feet in depth, — of course
"running across Cherry street, which was not then opened.

* Foot note in pencil, signed S. H., to a funeral eulogy in memory of Rev. Gilbert Tennent, preached in the Second Presbyterian Church, by Samuel Finley, D. D., 1764.

"When it was opened, seventeen feet were sold from the
"burying ground for the purpose of widening the street.
"Many years afterwards a strip of two and a half feet on the
"western side was purchased from Stephen Kingston. A
"brick building was erected on the north end of the burying
"ground by the congregation. To this building they removed
"from the corner of Arch and Third streets, and continued
"to worship there until the opening of the Church in Seventh
"street. After having been used for some years by schools
"and societies it was finally sold, with nineteen feet from the
"burying ground lot, from which all the dead were previously
"removed, chiefly with the consent of friends. The com-
"mittee who attended to this duty are all deceased but my-
"self. This burying ground has, therefore, been in use one
"hundred and fourteen (1750—1864) years, in which lie many
"of the great and good. There is no account, that I can find,
"of their owning any other burying ground prior to the pur-
"chase of this, but as there is a record of part of my grand-
"father's family being buried in the ground attached to 'the
"'new building,' in Fourth street, it is probable that the
"other members of the congregation, previous to the pur-
"chase in Arch street, were buried there, if not then re-
"moved. This ground not being considered large enough

"for the congregation, another lot, for the purpose of a bury-
"ing ground, was purchased on Eighth street.   This, being
"thought inconvenient, was resold.   Another burying ground
"was afterwards purchased between Noble and Buttonwood
"streets, which is still in use, from which, however, a portion
"on Buttonwood street has been sold, and houses erected
"thereon, as has since been done on Noble street."

"(Signed)   "SAMUEL HAZARD."

---

*From Report of a Special Committee of the Second Presbyterian
Church, exhibiting a general view of the financial concerns of
the Church.   Adopted April 12, 1832.*

"May 8th, 1826. — Bonds held by individuals in the Church: —

"Alexander Henry, ... $3,000 00
"John Stille, esq., ...   3,136 84
"Mary W. Brown, ...   500 00
"Catharine Lesley, ...   762 00

"These bonded debts arose from the erection of the Session House on
"Cherry street, and the purchase from the First Church of Northern Liberties
"of their congregational right to bury their dead in our Noble street ground,

"the limited size of which rendered it necessary that we should be in exclu-
"sive possession of the whole for our own use. This purchase was obtained
"for the sum of $1,500."

" The Burial Grounds have received much attention from the Board, in the
"economy of ground used for interment, and in the intelligent definition of the
"right of burial in the Ordinance of 1827. Forfeited spaces have been looked
"after and used, and all new graves ordered to be not less than nine feet
"deep, instead of six or seven, as formerly. A substantial new fence has been
"placed on the western side of the Noble street Ground, but on the eastern
"line a strong brick or stone wall is needed almost immediately, the ground
"on the east being opened as a public street, and graded considerably lower
"than the surface of the graveyard. For the erection of this wall the Board
"have sacredly pledged the proceeds of the sales of all vault scites in this
"ground, and a strong hope is indulged that the pew holders more immedi-
"ately interested in this graveyard will early secure a family burial vault,
"especially as by a late order of the Board the right of burial is continued in
"the family purchasing, without regard to pew right or church membership.
"The price of this ground at present is but $1 25 per square foot."

" It is hoped that when the sinking fund has accomplished its task of paying
"off the entire debt of the Church, that then the money from the sale of vault
"scites in the Arch street Ground will be applied to the erection of brick
"walls on the east and west side of this yard."

"THOMAS LATIMER,
"ISAAC SNOWDEN,
"JOHN WHITE,
"PETER LESLEY,

" *April 12th, 1832.*"   "*Committee.*"

BURYING GROUND IN MOUNT VERNON CEMETERY,

AND REMOVALS FROM ARCH STREET AND NOBLE STREET.

At a meeting of the regular members of the Second Presbyterian Church, held February 4, 1867, authority was given
by the congregation to sell the Burial Grounds belonging to
the Corporation, and a Committee was especially appointed
by the Trustees to take the necessary steps. This Committee
were empowered to remove the dead, and any tombs, monuments, etc., in said Grounds, to a more suitable and permanent location, and to make such removals at the expense of
the Church, and, in all cases, making with surviving relatives,
and friends of those who were interred therein, arrangements
satisfactory to them. The Report of this Committee was
approved by the Board of Trustees, and read at the Annual
Meeting of the regular members of the Church. This shows
that removals from the *Noble street Ground* numbered 1,129,
adults and children, a portion of which were taken in charge
by the relatives and friends, and re-interred in other cemeteries. The Committee superintended the largest portion of
the number, with one vault, three monuments, eleven tombs,

and two hundred and fourteen head and foot stones, to the
new burial plot of the Church in Mount Vernon Cemetery,
where sufficient ground for Church purposes had been
purchased.

" The very large number of vaults, tombs, and other im-
" provements in the *Arch street Ground* made it necessary for
" your Committee to have many interviews with, and consent
" of, the relatives of the dead therein, prior to giving an order
" for removing any from that Ground. The removals, under
" the care of your Committee, from the *Arch street Ground*,
" comprised a total of 1,479. Six new vaults and the re-
" erection of one monument, fifty tombs, one tablet, and two
" hundred and forty-three head and foot stones, to the new
" burial plot at Mount Vernon Cemetery, as, also, the building·
" of five new vaults in Laurel Hill Cemetery, and transferring
" thereto the remains formerly buried in the five original vaults
" in Arch street Ground."

" For information in regard to the transfer of the remains
" of the dead, individually, and of families, the papers and
" books, prepared with much care by your Committee, we
" believe will answer any and all queries on the subject."

" Your Committee have the satisfaction to remark that, as
" far as their knowledge extends, every family interested in

" the remains formerly in the Arch street Ground, as, also,
" those who had interest in the Noble street Ground, (except
" a very few persons connected with the Buttonwood street
" Church,) have expressed themselves perfectly satisfied with
" the transfer by us of their dead to our new Ground, and as
" also those families who took charge of their kin folk, and
" re-interred them in, and transferred their improvements into,
" other cemeteries, and received a money consideration or
" equivalent for their burial rights or vaults or improvements.
" The new plot in Mount Vernon Cemetery has been enclosed
" with a bronze rail and gate and granite posts."

CORNER STONES.

CORNER STONE OF THE CHURCH IN SEVENTH STREET, BELOW ARCH.

Before the corner stone was laid, the following inscription was placed within it : —

"The first building for the exclusive use of the Second Presbyterian Church "of Philadelphia was erected at the North-west corner of Mulberry and Dela- "ware Third streets, in the year 1750, and was enlarged in the year 1809. "In it the

"Rev. Gilbert Tennent, D. D.,   Rev. John N. Abeel,
"Rev. John Murray,   Rev. Jacob J. Janeway, D. D.,
"Rev. James Sproat, D. D.,   Rev. Thomas H. Skinner, D. D,
"Rev. Ashbel Green, D. D.,   Rev. Joseph Sanford, and
"Rev. Cornelius C. Cuyler, D. D.,

"Ministered successively, either as pastors or colleagues. The situation having "become unsuitable for a place of worship, the Congregation have selected this "in its stead; and now, at their request,

THIS CORNER STONE

OF

The Second Presbyterian Church in the City of Philadelphia,

IS LAID BY THE

Rev. CORNELIUS C. CUYLER, D. D.,

On the sixth day of September,

A. D. 1836.

"Andrew Jackson, being President of the U. S. of America.

"Joseph Ritner, Governor of the Commonwealth of Pennsylvania.

"John Swift, Mayor of the City of Philadelphia.

"Rev. Cornelius C. Cuyler, D. D., Pastor of the Church.

"The Presidency of the Board of Trustees vacant by the death of Robert "Ralston.

"Andrew Brown,	John V. Hart,	Edw. Smith,
Wm. Boyd,	John Harned,	Robert Smith,
Charles Chauncey,	Sam'l Hazard,	John Strawbridge,
Jas. H. Cole,	A. G. Jaudon,	Robt. Taylor,
Jacob David,	John K. Kane,	Benj. Stille, and
David S. Freeland,	Peter Lesley,	Dr. John White,
J. W. Gibbs,	David Mandeville,	
Chambers Gaw,	Chas. Macalester,	*Trustees.*"

"John K. Kane,	David S. Freeland,	Samuel Hazard,
Charles Chauncey,	John Strawbridge,	*Building Committee.*"

L

"Wm. Strickland, Architect.

"John Struthers & Son, Marble Masons.

"Henry Little, Carpenter.

"A. & E. Robbins, Bricklayers.

"Peter Prizer, Stone Mason."

"'Here will I dwell, for I have desired it.' Ps. cxxxii. 14.

"'In all places where I record my name, I will come unto thee, and I will "'bless thee.' Ex. xx. 24.

"'Establish Thou the work of our hands upon us.' Ps. xc. 17.

"'Save now, I beseech Thee, O Lord: O Lord, I beseech Thee, send now "'prosperity.' Ps. cxviii. 25."

"Within the stone are also deposited copies of

"The Constitution of the United States of America.

"The Constitution of the Commonwealth of Pennsylvania.

"The Confession of Faith of the Presbyterian Church in the United States.

"The Psalm Book of the same.

"The Charters of the Second Presbyterian Church in the City of Phila-"delphia.

"The Philadelphia Directory for 1835-1836.

"Dr. Green's Address at the interment of Robert Ralston.

"Dr. Cuyler's sermon on the death of Robert Ralston.

"'The Presbyterian,' of the 3rd September, 1836.

"'The Philadelphia Observer,' of the 1st September, 1836.

"The Annual Report of the Board of Education of the Presbyterian Church, "1836.

"The Annual Report of the Board of Missions of the same, 1836."

After the corner stone had been laid by the Rev. Dr. Cuyler, an address was delivered by the Rev. Dr. Green, prayer was offered by Rev. Wm. J. Gibson, and after the company assembled had sung the 132nd Psalm, the apostolical benediction was pronounced by the Rev. P. J. Sparrow.

CORNER STONE OF CHURCH TWENTY-FIRST AND WALNUT STREETS.

The corner stone of the Church at Twenty-first and Walnut streets was laid June 21, 1869, at the north-west corner of the building. The services were at five o'clock in the afternoon. A stage was provided with benches for the ladies, and a like stage with chairs for the gentlemen. The Rev. Albert Barnes, of the First Presbyterian Church, made the opening prayer. Dr. Matthew B. Grier read the 132nd Psalm, and 1 Cor., iii.: 9, 23. The 499th hymn was sung. Dr. Musgrave made an address. Mr. Theodore Cuyler then gave a history of the contents of the corner stone of the Church in Seventh street, which were removed in a dilapidated state. These and the new documents were then enclosed in a glass vase made for the purpose. The new documents were as follows: —

A book of portraits, containing: —

An engraved portrait of the President of the United States, Gen. U. S. Grant, with his autograph, written for this purpose.

An engraved portrait of the Governor of the State of Pennsylvania, Col. John W. Geary, with autograph, written for this purpose.

Photographic likeness of the Mayor of the City of Philadelphia, Hon. Daniel M. Fox, with autograph, written for this purpose.

The pastors of the Church: —

1. The portrait of Rev. George Whitefield, engraved.
2. Rev. Gilbert Tennent, engraved, and autograph sermon.
3. Rev. John Murray, engraved.

4. Rev. James Sproat, engraved, autograph.

5. Rev. Ashbel Green, engraved, autograph.

6. Rev. J. N. Abeel, photograph, with autograph.

7. Rev. Jacob J. Janeway, engraved, autograph.

8. Rev. Thomas H. Skinner, engraved, autograph.

9. Rev. Joseph Sanford, engraved, autograph.

10. Rev. Cornelius C. Cuyler, engraved, autograph.

11. Rev. Charles W. Shields, photograph, with autograph.

12. Rev. Elias R. Beadle, photograph, with autograph.

There were also in the corner stone as many of the MS. sermons of the pastors as could be obtained, one of them being Rev. Gilbert Tennent's. There were deposited specimens of the postal currency as follows : — 5 cent note, 10 cent note, 25 cent note, 50 cent note, a copy of the " Presby-"terian" newspaper of the last preceding issue, and of the " New York Observer." A picture of the old Church was also put in. A Sunday-school scholar gave two pennies, and a sewing woman deposited a dime in the stone. There were also accounts of the meeting of the two late General Assemblies. Besides the bottle containing these things there were two pieces of plate glass, on which were engraved, by fluoric acid, the following : —

FIRST PLATE.

" When time shall have crumbled to dust the stately walls which rise above
"this Corner Stone, or through other agencies it shall come again to human
" sight, an event not likely to occur until those who place it here, and gen-
" erations long succeeding them, shall have returned to dust, this Tablet will
" reveal the fact that on the twenty-first day of the month of June, in the year
" of Grace MDCCCLXIX the Congregation of the Second Presbyterian Church
" in the City of Philadelphia, trusting only in that Divine Grace which has
" rested upon this Church for one hundred and twenty-six years, did place
" this Corner Stone in the foundation of their new Church edifice at the South-
" east corner of Walnut street and Twenty-first street, having removed it from
" beneath their former edifice in Seventh street, south of Arch street."

SECOND PLATE.

" *Second Presbyterian Church in the City of Philadelphia.*

FOUNDED A. D. 1743.

Pastor. — Rev. E. R. BEADLE, D. D.

Ruling Elder. — THOMAS M. FREELAND.

BOARD OF TRUSTEES.

President. — THEODORE CUYLER.

Vice-President. — WILLIAM C. MORGAN.

Secretary. — JAMES D. KYD.

Treasurer. — GEORGE W. HALL.

Edward S. Clarke,

Uriah W. Stokes,

R. Case Clarke,

Charles F. Haseltine,

Wm. R. McAdam,

M. S. Stokes,

William Gallaher,

Thomas M. Freeland,

Richard Chambers,

Alexander Lesley,

John F. Taggart,

Pearson Yard,

James M. Earle,

Samuel L. Taylor,

H. Lenox Hodge, M. D.,

Furman Sheppard,

N. L. Hatfield,

Jas. H. Briscoe,

Adrian S. Clark.

BUILDING COMMITTEE.

Hugh L. Hodge, M. D.,

Charles F. Haseltine,

H. Lenox Hodge, M. D.,

The Pastor, *ex-officio*,

Theodore Cuyler,

Alex. Lesley,

U. W. Stokes, *Treasurer*.

Architect. — Henry A. Sims.

Superintendent. — John McClure.

Builder. — William Armstrong.

Glass Stainers and Engravers. — J. & G. H. Gibson."

The bottle and these glass plates were placed in the excavation of the old corner stone, and plaster of Paris was then poured around them and allowed to harden. Over this was deposited a slab of marble, and the whole covered with a block of excavated granite.

When all was in place, the usual ceremony of knocking the stone with the mallet was performed by the Pastor, Rev. Dr. Elias R. Beadle.   After this the Rev. Dr. Humphrey, of Calvary Church, offered prayer, and the services closed with the benediction by the Rev. Dr. Thomas De Witt, of the Dutch Reformed Church, of New York.

ORIGINAL SUBSCRIPTION

FOR LOT AND CHURCH AT WALNUT AND TWENTY-FIRST STREETS.

Copy of the original Subscription list.

"We, the subscribers, do engage to pay the sums affixed to our names on or "about May 8, 1868, for the purchase of a lot near Twenty-first and Walnut "streets, and towards the erection of a new place of public worship, and to "donate the same to the Second Presbyterian Church in Philadelphia."

"*Philadelphia, April 21, 1868.*"

(Signed)

Hugh L. Hodge, ...	$10,000 00	Paid in full.
Alexander Lesley, ...	1,000 00	"
Anna G. Hubbell, ...	1,000 00	"
Miss Hubbell, ...	100 00	"

Miss Lina Hubbell, ...	$ 100 00	Paid in full.
Mrs. Oswald Thompson, ...	250 00	"
Stephen H. Brooke, ...	1,000 00	"
Miss Caroline T. Cuyler, ...	100 00	"
Mrs. Joel Jones, ...	500 00	"
Charles Haseltine, ...	5,000 00	To be paid in instalments within 10 y'rs of which $1,000 paid.
H. Lenox Hodge, ...	5,000 00	To be paid in instalments within 10 y'rs of which $4,800 paid.
Mrs. H. Lenox Hodge, ...	1,200 00	Paid in full.
U. W. Stokes, ...	500 00	"
Mr. Kimball, ...	150 00	"
Mr. Theodore Cuyler, ...	2,500 00	"
The Misses Freeman, ...	141 00	"
Mr. R. Case Clark, ...	300 00	"
Thomas Brown, ...	100 00	"
Miss Elizabeth Chauncey, ...	1,000 00	"
Miss H. C. Ralston, ...	50 00	"

George W. Childs, ...	$1,000 00	Paid in full.
Miss Olmstead, ...	50 00	"
Mr. C. Cuyler Campbell, ...	50 00	"
Miss Rowland, ...	10 00	"
Mr. W. Dwight Bell, ...	250 00	"
Mr. James Bayard, ...	250 00	"
Judge Porter, ...	500 00	"
Miss Holland, ...	200 00	"
Miss Gwyneth, ...	5 00	"
Mrs. C. C. Cuyler, ...	100 00	"
Miss H. R. Earp, ...	100 00	"
Miss Massey, ...	20 00	"
Miss Cole, ...	5 00	"
Mr. Edward S. Clarke, ...	500 00	"
Mrs. Francis E. Koons, ...	100 00	"
Mrs. Stephen Colwell, ...	100 00	"
Miss L. Harriet, ...	25 00	"
H. A Mariner, ...	5 75	"
Cash (per H. A. Mariner), ...	4 25	"
Miss Agnes Reynolds, ...	5 00	"

Mr. & Mrs. Wm. Gallaher, ...	$250 00	Paid in full.
Mrs. Harmer, ...	50 00	"
Miss Burkhart, ...	5 00	"
Dr. Edward Peace, ...	100 00	"
Mrs. R. H. Smith and daughters, ...	50 00	"
Mr. William Alex. Smith, ...	100 00	"
Miss Mary Rice, ...	25 00	"
Mr. H. W. Pitkin, ...	300 00	"
Mr. C. E. Claghorn, ...	250 00	"
Mrs. Mayfield, ...	50 00	"
M. Baird & Co., ...	100 00	"
Miss J. S. Woolsey, ...	100 00	"